Learning to Use Written Language

—

Lessons from the South Bay Writing Project

Grades 1–3

by Iris M. Tiedt and Nora G. Ho

Fearon Teacher Aids
a division of
David S. Lake Publishers
Belmont, California 94002

Lesson plans are based on the contributions of the following teachers:

    Sally Beste

    Maria Buchinski

    Kathleen M. Ledger

    Anne Marie Plonka

    Patricia Schuesler

    Mildred Taylor

Cover and book illustrator: Duane Bibby

Entire contents copyright © 1987 by David S. Lake Publishers, 19 Davis Drive, Belmont, California 94002. Permission is hereby granted to reproduce designated materials in this book for noncommercial classroom and individual use.

ISBN 0-8224-4267-1

Printed in the United States of America

1. 9 8 7 6 5 4 3 2 1

Contents

Introduction *1*
Planning a Good Writing Lesson *3*
SAFE Lesson Plan *5*
Tips for Organizing Your Writing Program *6*

Unit 1: Beginning with Oral Expression *9*
SAFE Lesson Plans
   Walnut-Shell Animals *10*
   Classifying Animals *13*
   Can I Keep Him? *14*
   What's in a Picture? *16*
Additional Writing Activities *18*

Unit 2: Acting Out for Learning *19*
SAFE Lesson Plans
   Naming Words *20*
   Pantomime *22*
   Tell It in Sequence *23*
   New Dialogue for an Old Story *25*
   Adventure Game *27*
Additional Writing Activities *30*

Unit 3: From Listening to Writing *31*
SAFE Lesson Plans
   Snowy Day *32*
   Character Descriptions *34*
   Ask Me Again *36*
   Picture This *39*
Additional Writing Activities *42*

Unit 4: I Can Write! *43*
SAFE Lesson Plans
   Words to Describe *44*
   Making an Alphabet Book *47*
   Echoic Words *49*
   Descriptive Phrases Chart *51*
Additional Writing Activities *53*

Unit 5: Getting into Narrative Writing *55*
SAFE Lesson Plans
   Happiness Is . . . *56*
   Teddy Bear Picnic *57*
   From Fear to Story *59*
   Taking Another Point of View *62*
Additional Writing Activities *64*

Unit 6: Expository Writing *65*
SAFE Lesson Plans
   Letter Writing *66*
   Mapping a Paragraph *69*
   Grocery Shopping *72*
   Snail Articles *74*
Additional Writing Activities *76*

Unit 7: Editing Your Writing *77*
SAFE Lesson Plans
   Capital Letters *78*
   Punctuation *80*
   My Own Personal Dictionary *81*
   Expanding Sentences *82*
   Checking on Our Writing *84*
Additional Writing Activities *86*
The Lesson Generator *87*
Children's Books Cited in This Text *90*
Reading Aloud *91*

Introduction

Kids Can Write!

Children prepare to write as they begin to learn language. As toddlers—even as infants—they already listen to language around them, and their active brains absorb the sounds of language. Soon they try to make meaningful sounds themselves. Gradually they make sounds they learn to associate with certain meanings—for example, "ma-ma" and "da-da." We respond encouragingly, and the child talks and talks and talks!

Most children are self-motivated to learn language. They listen and practice during all their waking hours. Without instruction, they observe how the system of language works. They notice patterns, the way words go together to make sense.

The two-year-old creates brief but meaningful sentences: "Daddy up. Johnny go. All gone truck." But this child grammar evolves as the child gains a greater understanding of grammar. The four-year-old's sentences are fuller than the two-year-old's: "Give me the ball, Meggie, or I'll tell Mommy." By the time children enter kindergarten, they are chattering fluently, using a wide range of grammatical structures.

Children compose sentences all the time, running them freely through their "grammar machines" so the sentences make sense to them. The eight-year-old's sentences are quite complex: "Hey, Tom, ask your dad if you can come over to my house after school tomorrow." Tom immediately decodes the sentence, runs to ask his dad, and is back to report, "Yeah, Kurt, he says it will be okay as long as I come home in time for supper." The children may not know the terms of grammar—nouns, verbs, adjectives, dependent clauses, or compound sentences. But they intuitively apply complex rules of grammar as they compose a variety of sentences during conversation.

Oral language experiences prepare children to write. Children draw on their knowledge of words and concepts, such as the ideas they remember from books read aloud to them, or concepts they have talked about with friends or family. Stored in their brains is a wealth of knowledge that we will help them tap as they begin to write.

We of the South Bay Writing Project have written this book to help you:

- Use oral language to support writing
- Build children's self-esteem through writing
- Guide students to write successfully
- Make use of reading and writing connections
- Show young writers how to improve their writing

The writing lessons in this book are grouped into seven units, arranged sequentially to complement the development of writing skills. Each unit contains from three to six separate writing lessons. These writing lessons have been developed and written by teachers, the same teachers who use these lessons in their own classrooms.

A lesson plan directed to the teacher introduces each writing lesson. In most cases, a reproducible page used for that lesson and directed to the student follows the lesson plan page. The lesson plan format may be adapted to numerous other writing activities of your own design. Using the lessons in this book will help you plan writing lessons of your own that both you and your students will enjoy, lessons that will help them grow as writers.

About the South Bay Writing Project

The South Bay Writing Project was created in 1976 as part of the California Writing Project and the National Writing Project. The organization is located at San Jose State University in San Jose, California. It serves students, teachers, and schools in the southern portion of the Bay Area.

The South Bay Writing Project follows the two major thrusts of the writing project model: a summer writing institute that trains K-14 teacher consultants, and ongoing staff development for local teachers. In addition, the project has innovated other activities designed to stimulate and to improve student writing, such as the Young Writers' Conference and a Computers in Language Arts Conference.

Through our work with the South Bay Writing Project, we are always learning more about how to teach writing. We want to share some of these principles with you.

Writing is thinking
Thinking and expressing thoughts develop together from the time of a child's birth. As children become aware of written language, they are motivated to express their ideas in writing. Their writing reveals what they are thinking about. Putting thoughts in writing helps children clarify and organize their thinking.

Oral language provides the foundation for writing
Children develop oral language before they work with written language. This prior knowledge of vocabulary and ideas is essential to successful writing. We need to expose children to concepts and experiences so they have something to say, and the tools with which to say it before we ask them to write.

Children learn to write by reading
Through listening to stories and reading what others write, children develop a sense of story or a sense of how others make a statement. By observing the writing of skilled authors, students learn ways to improve their own writing. Improving writing is a matter of grammar and style.

Children learn to write by writing
In order to learn to write with ease, children need to write frequently. They can write lists, notes, questions, answers to questions, conversations, paragraphs, memories, stories, reports, poems, and so on. They will benefit from writing on a daily basis.

We can teach young writers to improve their writing abilities
The ability to write well comes from practice, persistence, and the discovery that writing is enjoyable. We can help students find this joy by making them feel comfortable with writing, comfortable enough to practice and persevere. We must start by accepting the beginning writers' early efforts, praising students for what they have achieved. By talking about writing and by observing the writing of others, young writers will learn how to make their writing more effective. We can guide them to experiment with new styles, new forms, and more sophisticated ways of writing.

This book contains writing lessons that will help you teach writing based on these principles. You can also create writing lessons of your own using interesting ideas that you already have. The rest of this introduction shows you how to create lessons that engage students in the writing process.

Planning a Good Writing Lesson

The best writing lesson begins with objectives. Think about what you want your students to learn during the course of that lesson. Your objectives should be specific, but they may also be flexible.

Objectives may reflect what you expect students to demonstrate during the lesson. Or they may tell what you expect students to be able to accomplish as a result of the lesson. Objectives may also describe what skills the lesson allows students to practice. Here are some examples of objectives.

Students will:
1. Discuss a controversial issue and express an opinion.
2. Recognize adjectives.
3. Write an expository paragraph.
4. Tell a story about a real event.
5. Use transitions as they relate a sequence of events.
6. Identify the point of view in a story.
7. Proofread other students' stories.
8. Suggest ways to improve a composition.

A lesson plan usually has a few related objectives. When you write your own lessons, you will want to create a plan that incorporates the objectives you have selected. List your objectives and keep them in mind during the lesson.

Each lesson plan in this book has four essential components: the **s**timulus (or prewriting activity), the main **a**ctivity, the **f**ollow-up activity, and the **e**valuation. The key words of this plan form the acronym "SAFE." Let's take a look at each component of the SAFE Lesson Plan.

Stimulus

Any part of the lesson that occurs before students write, and that is intended to stimulate writing, may be considered the stimulus. Listening to a story read aloud often stimulates writing. Other stimulus activities include watching a film, observing an unusual object, or participating in a field trip. The stimulus activities in this book almost always include group discussion and preparation for the main activity.

Activity

The main activity is the performance by the students. Usually this performance will be a form of writing. Occasionally the activity may be oral, designed to parallel the writing program.

Students may write (or present orally) paragraphs, stories, reports, letters, poems, skits, dialogues, essays, and so on. They may perform skits or role-play situations they envision. In short, the lessons in this book cover a wide variety of forms as main activities.

Follow-up

The follow-up activity is defined as whatever occurs after the main activity. It should be designed to support the main activity. Usually the follow-up will be a postwriting activity.

Postwriting activities are highly motivating and encourage further writing, so they are important to the success of a particular lesson. The postwriting activities in this book usually involve students sharing their stories or compositions, editing or correcting surface errors, rewriting, and completing stories begun.

Evaluation

Teachers are encouraged to use a variety of techniques to evaluate students' writing. Sometimes it is more appropriate for students to evaluate each other's work than for the teacher to be the sole judge. Since all writers need frequent practice, a teacher cannot be expected to read everything that his or her students write. Student evaluations give teachers a chance to share the load, but, more importantly, they give students an opportunity to develop critical judgment and an appreciation for the task of writing.

The teacher (and often the students) should evaluate a lesson in terms of the objectives. Sometimes the teacher may evaluate by observing student participation. Small groups of students evaluate by choosing a composition they consider the best among several. The teacher may also collect students' papers to read aloud and discuss with the class. At other times, teachers will want to collect papers, write comments on the papers, and assign grades.

Remember that the word "evaluation" contains the word "value." Emphasize the worth of each writing attempt. By doing so, you will build students' self-esteem and ensure that students continue writing.

Some Concluding Remarks on the SAFE Lesson Plans
This book contains 32 teacher-written, classroom-tested SAFE Lesson Plans. Each SAFE Lesson Plan has a complete, fully prepared, self-contained lesson. You can select the lesson plans most appropriate for your class, and just follow the step-by-step instructions.

This book has a second purpose. We hope that teachers will adapt the "SAFE" components (**s**timulus, **a**ctivity, **f**ollow-up, and **e**valuation) to their own writing lessons for use in the classroom. We have even supplied a blank lesson plan (see page 5) to facilitate planning. First try some of the SAFE Lesson Plans in this book. Then create your own SAFE Lesson Plans, and share them with your colleagues.

Dear Parents:

I am pleased to have your child in my room this year. We will be sharing many exciting learning experiences.

We will be making a special effort to improve writing skills. I want you to understand some of the things we will be doing.

1. All children will keep a writing portfolio (folder) in which to save writing done each day. This visible record of what they have achieved will be shared with you during conferences and bound periodically as a personal anthology for each student.

2. We will take a writing sample soon to serve as a benchmark for each student. At the end of the year we will take another sample. Comparing these samples will show you and your child the growth made during the year.

3. Children will learn many different forms of writing—stories, reports, poems, plays. They will also write for different purposes—to ask for information, to express feelings, to summarize what they have learned. Some of their writing will be done in the social studies or other subject areas.

4. Children will write for different audiences—other children, themselves, you, an editor. By speaking to other people through writing, they are acquiring a "voice," a sense of themselves as having something to say. They will build their confidence and self-esteem.

5. We will talk about good writing and observe writing in books we read. Children will learn to edit their writing to improve word usage, style, and mechanics. Important selections (not everything they write) will go through several drafts as students polish their writing for publication in some way. This writing will be evaluated for grades to go on report cards.

I hope to assist the children in growing as writers and to enjoy the process.

Cordially yours,

Unit 1

Beginning with Oral Expression

Oral language is the foundation for writing; it is an essential readiness skill. Oral language is the most common means of expression, the first mode a child learns, and usually the means in which students feel most secure. Oral language experiences should challenge students to elaborate and extend the language patterns they already know.

SAFE Lesson Plan

Walnut-Shell Animals

Objectives

Students will:
1. Follow written and pictorial directions to construct an art project.
2. Create stories to tell.
3. Write or dictate a sentence about the walnut-shell animals they have constructed.

Materials

"Walnut-Shell Animals" activity sheets (pp. 11–12)
walnut shell halves
poster paint or felt-tipped markers
construction paper
scissors
liquid white glue
string
blank paper

Stimulus

Make at least two walnut-shell animals—a turtle and a mouse—according to the activity sheets. You may also wish to make a different animal to show how the directions on the activity sheet may be altered, using a little creativity. Display the animals for the class to see. Let the students make up stories to tell about the animals.

Activity

1. Make several copies of each activity sheet. Allow students to choose which animal they wish to make. (For some primary students, it may be advisable to have everyone in the class make either turtles or mice. With more advanced students, however, you may even encourage them to make different animals than those described on the activity sheets.)
2. Students may follow the written and/or pictorial directions on the activity sheets to make their walnut-shell animals. With classes of young students, you may have to cut out construction paper body parts ahead of time.
3. Give each student a sheet of blank paper. Have students draw a scene in which to place the walnut-shell animals.
4. Have each student tell a brief story about her or his animal. Students may write a sentence (or dictate a sentence to be written) on the picture.

Follow-up

Line up the pictures and the walnut-shell animals on tables or cabinets. For a less temporary display, glue the walnut-shell animals onto their pictures, and tack the pictures on a bulletin board. The walnut-shell animal pictures make a good display for a classroom open house.

Evaluation

Observe student participation. Encourage students to envision their animals in unusual places and then to depict those places in their drawings and stories.

Activity Sheet *Walnut-Shell Animals: Turtle*

1. Color the shell.
   Use paint or a marker.

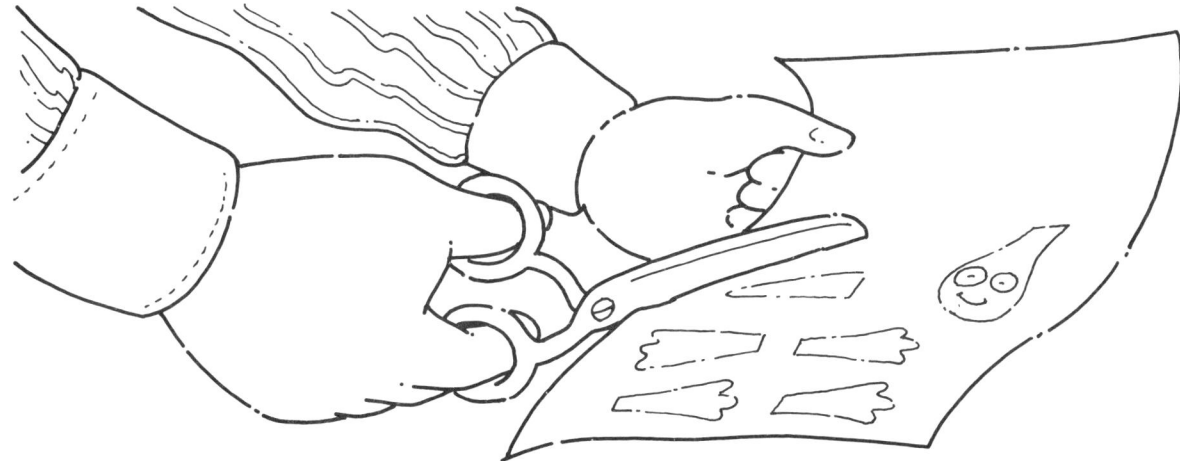

2. Cut out a paper head, a tail, and feet.

3. Glue the body parts to the shell.

Activity Sheet *Walnut-Shell Animals: Mouse*

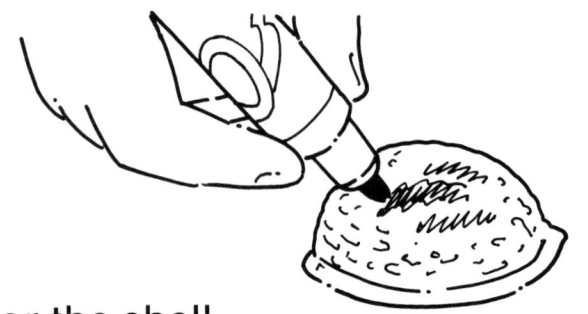 

1. Color the shell.
   Use paint or a marker.

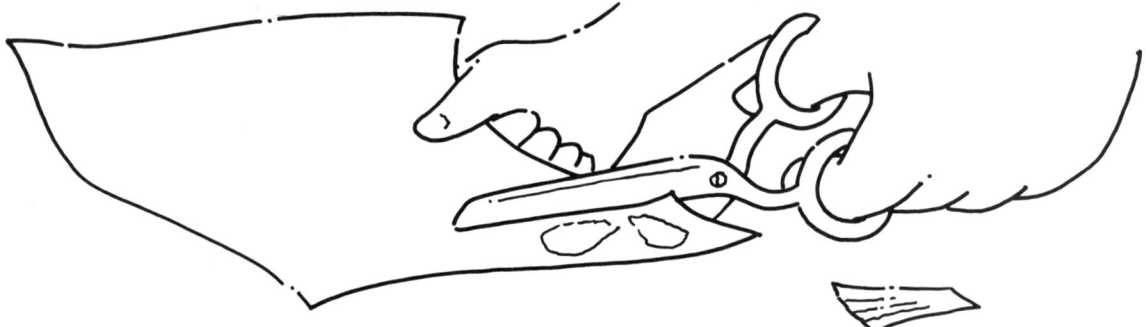

2. Cut out paper ears, whiskers, and eyes.

3. Glue the body parts to the shell.

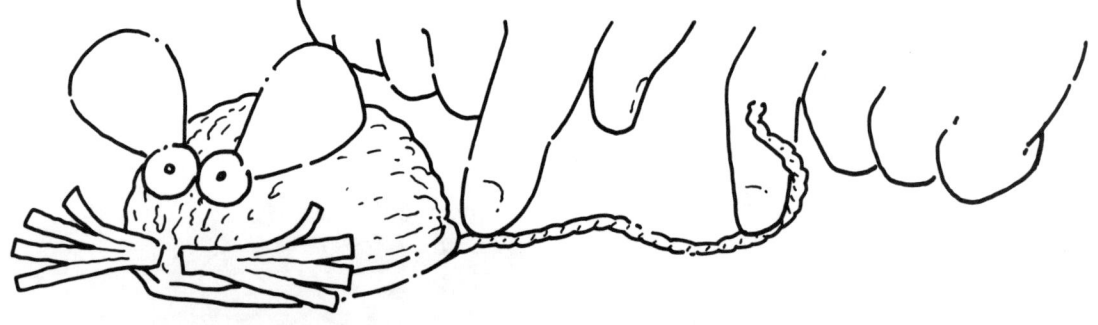

4. Cut a piece of string.
   Glue it to the shell to make a tail.

SAFE Lesson Plan — # Classifying Animals

Objectives

Students will:
1. Demonstrate good listening skills by retelling a story in sequence.
2. Classify animals according to general habitat.
3. Tell about unusual animals they have seen in nature.

Materials

any storybook that describes a variety of animals, such as *Animals Should Definitely Not Wear Clothes*, by Judi Barrett, or *You Don't Look Like Your Mother*, by Aileen Fisher

Stimulus

Read the story aloud to the class. Ask a few students to retell the events of the story in sequence. Reread the story and have the students join in, saying aloud the parts they remember.

Activity

1. Draw a Venn diagram on the chalkboard. Label the circles as shown below.

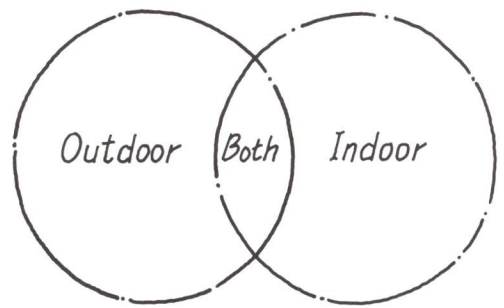

2. Ask the class which animals in the story live outdoors, which live indoors, and which live both outdoors and indoors. List the animals on the Venn diagram exactly as the students tell you. If a listing is inappropriate, call attention to it and ask the students to think again about this animal's habitat. Correct all inappropriate listings.

Follow-up

Ask the students about animals they have seen in the animals' natural habitats. Give each student an opportunity to tell about the most unusual animal she or he has seen in nature.

Evaluation

Be supportive and patient as students relate their stories verbally. Encourage students to be informative yet succinct. With reluctant students, ask specific questions about the animals and their habitats.

SAFE Lesson Plan   *Can I Keep Him?*

Objectives

Students will:
1. Discuss characteristics of various animals as pets.
2. Complete a sentence about a favorite animal.

Materials

Can I Keep Him?, by Steven Kellogg
books and/or magazines with pictures of animals
"Can I Keep Him?" activity sheet (p. 15)
pencils
crayons

Stimulus

Read *Can I Keep Him?* aloud to the class. Discuss the story. Then ask the students to tell the class about any pets they might have at home.

Activity

1. Show the class various pictures of animals. Ask them to identify the animals and to describe characteristics of each animal. Then ask them which animals would make good pets and why. Make a list on the chalkboard of some animals they mention. Next to each animal listed, jot down the reasons mentioned for that animal's being a good pet.

> turkey — When you get tired of it you can eat it.
> snake — You can scare your little brother with it.
> mouse — It is soft and cute.

2. Give each student a copy of the activity sheet. Ask students to complete the sentence on the activity sheet, naming their favorite animal and explaining why they would like to have that animal as a pet. You may wish to suggest that students choose animals other than those they actually have as pets. In this way, all students will use their imaginations.

Follow-up

Have each student draw a picture of the preferred animal. Suggest that students draw pictures that show the animals as pets in the students' homes.

Evaluation

Display the completed activity sheets on the bulletin board. Give the students an opportunity to read each other's sentences and comment verbally on the pictures.

Activity Sheet *Can I Keep Him?*

I would like to keep a _____

because _____

15

SAFE Lesson Plan # *What's in a Picture?*

Objective

Students will study a picture and dictate what they see in the picture.

Materials

"What's in a Picture?" activity sheet (p. 17), or any interesting, thought-provoking picture or photograph
lined paper
pencils

Stimulus

This lesson works best if you have volunteer helpers or a teacher's aide in the classroom, since it requires that the teacher (or aide or volunteers) offer individual attention to each student. Give each student a copy of the activity sheet or other picture. Explain that the students may look at the picture but may not discuss it with each other.

Activity

1. Call each student to meet with you individually. (The aide or volunteers may help you with this.) Ask the student to tell you what she or he sees in the picture. To stimulate expression, ask questions such as "What (or who) do you see in the picture?" "Where are they?" "What are they doing?" "Why are they doing this?" Write the student's responses on a sheet of lined paper.

2. Have the students rewrite their responses on another sheet of paper. They may reword or rearrange their sentences to make better sense.

Follow-up

Display the students' papers along with the picture on the bulletin board. Later, bind the papers in a class book so the students may reread them as a free-time activity.

Evaluation

Students may comment on each other's papers as they read them. Praise students who freely express what they see in the picture.

Activity Sheet # What's in a Picture?

Additional Writing Activities for Unit 1

Choric Speaking
Ask students to say the following exclamatory sentence together: "I can't believe I ate the whole thing!" Then ask them to try saying the sentence as if they were laughing. Next, ask them to try saying it as if they were afraid; then, as if they were angry. Suggest other variations, and give the students an opportunity to experiment with intonation on their own.

Voice Choir
Borrow an anthology of songs and poetry from the library. Find short songs and poems that are familiar or easy to learn, and ones that are fun to sing or to recite. Write the words on the chalkboard or on poster board, and have the class sing the song or recite the poem together in a singsong fashion. Examples are: "Poor Old Woman," "Eensy, Weensy Spider," "This Old Man," and "I Never Saw a Purple Cow."

Group Talk
Divide the class into groups of three students each. Give the class a word, such as "apple," "fence," or "pencil." Then give the students a few moments to collect their thoughts about the topic word. Allow each group a given amount of time (such as a minute) to speak on that topic. The students in each group can take turns speaking as quickly as they can, filling the given time with as meaningful discussion as possible about the topic. Signal "Go!" to begin their talk and "Stop!" to end it.

Group Stories
Have students pair up. Each partner will tell a true story about something that happened to her or him a long time ago, while the other person listens. The listener then retells the partner's story as accurately as possible, and the partner makes corrections. Have each student choose a new partner and retell the original partner's story to the new partner.

Rumors
Divide the class into about five groups. Have one student from each group whisper a long sentence to another student in the group. That student will then whisper the sentence to another student. The game continues until each student in the group has heard the sentence. Ask the last student to say the sentence aloud and compare it with the original sentence whispered by the first player.

Unit 2

Acting Out for Learning

Drama gives children an opportunity to express themselves spontaneously and creatively. It also gives them an opportunity to experiment using their voices and movement. Since there is no right or wrong way to interpret written words, a child can feel free to act out an idea or a thought without fear of rejection. This helps build self-esteem, which is critical to a child's success with writing.

SAFE Lesson Plan *Naming Words*

Objectives

Students will:
1. Compose sentences using naming words (nouns).
2. Name nouns and use them in sentences.

Materials

"Naming Words" activity cards (p. 21)
tagboard
scissors
index cards
sentence strips
lined paper
pencils

Stimulus

1. Define *noun* for the class. Explain that nouns are naming words, and give some examples.
2. Make a set of activity cards on tagboard. Cut apart the cards.
3. Hold up the cards, one at a time. Have students read the words aloud and tell what each word (in its noun form) means. For each word, ask a student to point to an object in the classroom or to draw a picture of an object that exemplifies the word.

Activity

1. Have students collectively compose sentences using the naming words written on the activity cards. Encourage them to use more than one of the naming words in a sentence. (Examples: The pig is wearing a vest; a bird put a twig in the nest.) Write the sentences on the chalkboard.
2. Ask students to copy the sentences on paper and to circle each naming word.

Follow-up

Prepare a bulletin board with the caption "Nouns Are Naming Words." Have students identify other naming words. Write each word on a small index card. Have students compose sentences using these words. Write their sentences on sentence strips. Pin the index cards and sentence strips on the bulletin board.

Evaluation

Observe student participation. Make sure that students use the naming words as nouns; many nouns may also serve as other parts of speech. You need not explain this complexity to the class; simply suggest other ways to use the words as nouns.

Variation

Make two sets of activity cards, each one on tagboard of a different color. Cut apart the cards. Place them in a learning center, and have the students play a memory game with the cards. They may play individually, in pairs, or in teams. Students will line up the cards in rows, facedown, after shuffling them. In turn, each student draws two cards at a time, trying to get a matched pair. If the cards do not match, the student puts them back in position. If they match, the student keeps the cards and takes another turn. Students try to remember where the cards are positioned.

Activity Cards *Naming Words*

bat	cat	hat
mat	bug	jug
rug	jig	pig
twig	wig	nest
	pest	vest

21

SAFE Lesson Plan *Pantomime*

Objectives

Students will:
1. Act out action words (verbs).
2. Guess action words acted out by others.
3. Write a sentence using an action word.

Materials

lined paper
pencils

Stimulus

1. Write the following words on the chalkboard: sit, stand, walk, crawl, dig, lift, carry, eat, talk, write.
2. Act out one of the words. Ask the students to name the word you have just acted out. Have one student go to the chalkboard and point out the word.
3. Explain that all of the words on the chalkboard are action words. These words tell what we do or tell about motion.

Activity

1. Explain that to *pantomime* is to act out an idea or a thought using gestures and motions but without words or other vocal sounds.
2. Select a student. Whisper one of the chalkboard action words to the student. That student acts out the action word for the class, and the other students must try to guess the word. Continue the activity until each student has had a chance to act out a word.
3. Have each student choose an action word from the list on the chalkboard and write a sentence using that word. Encourage the students to express a thought or an idea in each sentence. (Example: The children dig in the sand at the seashore.) More advanced students may write a sentence for each of four or five action words or they may write a sentence that uses two or three action words. You may also have advanced students write a longer scenario based on one action sentence.

Follow-up

1. Each student may draw a picture to illustrate the sentence (or scenario) she or he has written.
2. Prepare a bulletin board with the following caption: Action Words! Allow students to tack their papers to the board as they complete the activity.

Evaluation

Observe student participation during the pantomime portion of this activity. Encourage students to think of new ways to act out the words. Give students an opportunity to read each other's sentences.

SAFE Lesson Plan ## *Tell It in Sequence*

Objectives

Students will:
1. Collectively write a short story or narrative.
2. Retell a story or narrative in the correct sequence.

Materials

pumpkins
pencils
felt-tipped markers
"Tell It in Sequence" activity sheet (p. 24)

Stimulus

1. Give each student a pumpkin. Have the students create jack-o'-lantern faces on their pumpkins using pencils first and then felt-tipped markers.
2. Have the students share stories about their pumpkins, about carving jack-o'-lanterns, about growing pumpkins, or about Halloween.

Activity

1. Divide the class into small groups. Have each group create a story or narrative to tell the rest of the class. Suggest the following: a Halloween story, a narrative that tells how to make a Halloween costume, a step-by-step guide to pumpkin-carving, or a narrative about how to have a safe Halloween.
2. After the group has decided on the narrative or story, the students may dictate it to you (or to an aide or volunteer).
3. Give each student a copy of the activity sheet. Have each group make a continuing story or narrative, copying one or two sentences of their story or narrative on each activity sheet. Students should not number their pages to indicate the order.

Follow-up

1. Have one student from each group read the collectively written, continuing story or narrative.
2. Have the groups share their stories and narratives. Have one student in the group jumble the pages of the story or narrative and give them to a student in another group to read in sequence.

Evaluation

Encourage students to participate equally. Praise those groups whose stories or narratives reflect such a collective effort. Comment on those stories or narratives that are difficult to follow out of sequence.

Activity Sheet — *Tell It in Sequence*

SAFE Lesson Plan *Adventure Game*

Objectives

Students will:
1. As a group, choose a theme for a game board and write brief adventure scenarios.
2. Follow written rules to plan a board game.
3. Act out adventure situations.

Materials

Jumanji, by Chris Van Allsburg
"Adventure Game" game board and playing cards (pp. 28-29)
scissors
pencils
crayons or felt-tipped markers
dice (numbered 1-6)
game markers

Stimulus

1. Have students tell what kinds of games they like to play during their free time. Ask if they like to play board games, and which ones are their favorites.
2. Read *Jumanji* aloud to the class. Discuss the story, the game board rules, and the situations that arose during the game.
3. Lead a discussion of other adventure situations that might arise in the jungle. Discuss other adventures besides being in the jungle.

Activity

1. Divide the class into small groups. Give each group a copy of the game board and playing cards.
2. Have students in each group choose a theme for their adventure game. Some suggestions for adventure themes are the wild west, pirates, the circus, arctic exploration, deep sea exploration, and time travel. Each group will then complete a set of game cards for their adventure game, posing an adventure situation for each card, appropriate both to the card and to the theme. Students must be able to act out each adventure situation, which should be similar to those situations in the book *Jumanji*. Give a few examples. Review these activity directions with the class, and make sure they understand the assignment.
3. When they have completed their set of cards, have one student in each group cut apart the cards.
4. Finally, have students in each group illustrate their game board and their cards to depict the theme of the game.

Follow-up

Have the groups exchange game boards and cards. Give each group a set of game markers and a die. Have students roll the die; the student with the highest number rolls first and play continues clockwise. Students move their markers the number of spaces indicated. When a player lands on a space that reads "Draw a card," the player takes a card from the stack of shuffled cards, placed facedown. The player reads the card and the others in the group momentarily act out the situation. Play continues until one player reaches the finish space.

Evaluation

Circulate through the classroom as students are writing their game board cards. Offer help as needed. Read the game board cards. Comment on the uniqueness and the appropriateness of the situations posed. Make sure situations can be acted out.

Game Board *Adventure Game*

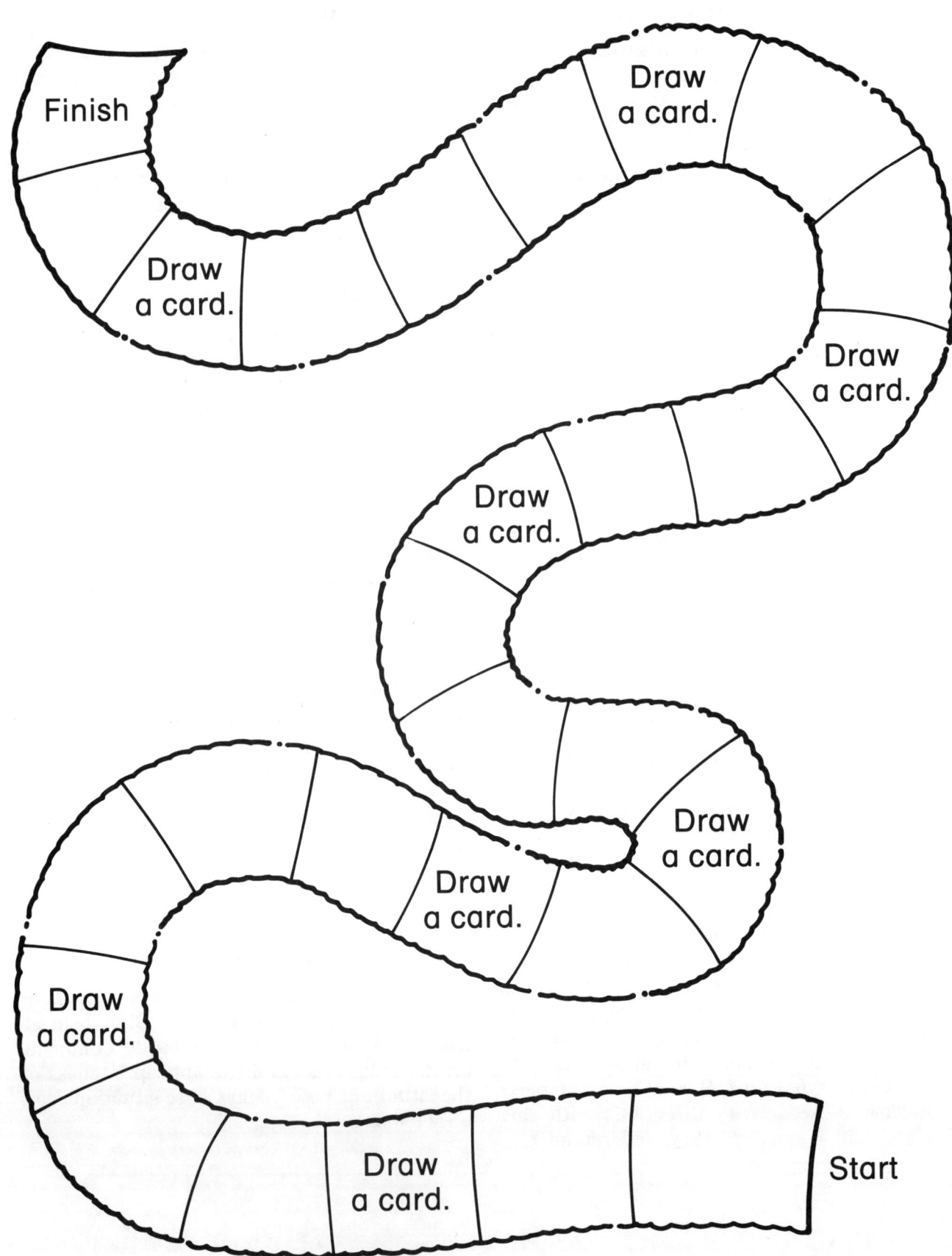

28

Playing Cards *Adventure Game*

Write a brief adventure situation for each card. Make sure the situation fits the action that follows. Also make sure the situation fits the theme of your game.

Take another turn.	Lose one turn.
Go back one space.	Go back two spaces.
Go back three spaces.	Go back to "start."
Advance one space.	Advance two spaces.

Additional Writing Activities for Unit 2

Where Did You Go Last Sunday?
Divide the class into groups of five or six students. Each group will form a circle, and one person in each circle will begin the game by asking the player to his or her left, "Where did you go last Sunday?" The player will respond with an imaginary answer such as "Last Sunday I flew over the ocean to Madrid." After responding, that player then asks the next player, "Where did you go last Sunday?" The game continues, each player trying to give a more fantastic response than the last.

Being Parents
Divide the class into small groups. Have the students role-play their parents or grandparents and converse with each other about "their children." Afterwards, bring the class together and discuss how it feels to be in charge of a family. Discuss the responsibilities that come with being in charge of a family.

Pantomime
Have students take turns pantomiming a familiar action, such as combing their hair in front of a mirror or hanging clothes on a clothesline. The rest of the class tries to guess the action. The first person to guess correctly becomes the next actor.

Scroll Theater
Read a storybook such as *Peter Pan* (short, storybook version) aloud to the class. Have students illustrate the story, representing the major events of the story. Tape the drawings together end-to-end to form a scroll, and attach each end of the scroll to a broom handle. You or the students can retell the story and turn the pictures on the scroll.

Divide the class into small groups. Have each group create a scroll for a familiar story. The groups can present their stories and show the scrolled illustrations to each other in a theater setting.

Role-play
Have students collectively create a situation for role-playing. (The situation should involve several people.) Ask who, what, where, when, and why questions to get the students to describe the situation. Clarify the plot. Then have students volunteer to play the characters, making up appropriate dialogue as they go along. After students have practiced role-playing in a large-group setting, have them work in small groups on their own, devising role-play situations to present to the class. Eventually, students will be able to write each situation into a play.

Puppetry
Have students make simple finger puppets or stick puppets. Have them work in pairs, using their puppets to converse with each other. Then divide the class into small groups and have each group plan a short skit to be acted out by their puppets. Suggest they act out fables that teach a lesson. Use a desk or a large box as a puppet stage. Students may use masks made from paper plates instead of puppets.

Unit 3

From Listening to Writing

Listening skills are important at every grade level, but they are especially important for primary students, who are still learning to adapt to the educational environment. Storytelling is an excellent way to encourage good listening skills. It comes naturally to most children. Through telling or reading stories, students will become aware of plot, characterization, and other elements of fiction.

Reading a good book aloud to the class is a good way to begin a writing lesson. Reading promotes the language skills necessary for writing. When you read aloud to students—or when they read aloud—they develop an ear for good writing. Reading also stimulates thought and offers a topic for discussion.

SAFE Lesson Plan *Snowy Day*

Objectives

Students will:
1. Retell a story in sequence.
2. Tell whether they liked or disliked the story.
3. Write two sentences to express an opinion of a story.

Materials

The Snowy Day, by Ezra Jack Keats
"Snowy Day" activity sheet (p. 33)
plain white paper
pencils
scissors (blunt-end scissors are fine)

Stimulus

1. Read *The Snowy Day* aloud to the class.
2. Discuss the story. Also discuss the snow, cold weather, and the coming of winter. If you live in a climate that does not experience dramatic season changes, bring picture books to show what a typical cold-climate winter might look like.
3. Call on several students to recount the events in *The Snowy Day*, in sequence.
4. Ask students to tell whether they liked or disliked the story and why. Write some of their reasons on the chalkboard.

Activity

Give each student a copy of the activity sheet. The students may work independently to complete the page. Urge students to think carefully before they write, and allow about ten minutes for the writing activity.

Follow-up

1. Have students read their sentences to the class.
2. Give each student a couple of sheets of blank white paper and a pair of scissors. Show students how to fold the paper in half, in thirds, and to cut the folded paper to make a unique snowflake design.

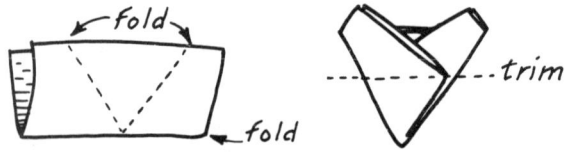

3. Display the activity sheets and the snowflakes on a bulletin board. This makes a good display for an open-house event.

Evaluation

Praise students' efforts at sentence writing. Ask questions to confirm a student's opinion or to encourage the student to be more detailed or informative.

Variations

In addition to reading *The Snowy Day*, show the film by the same title (Weston Woods). Check with your district film library or your public library.

Activity Sheet *Snowy Day*

Complete the sentence below about the story *The Snowy Day*. Write another sentence as an explanation.

I liked this story because _____

SAFE Lesson Plan — *Character Description*

Objectives

Students will:
1. Distinguish physical traits and personality traits.
2. Identify character (personality) traits in story characters.
3. Write a short paragraph to describe a story character.

Materials

any version of the story "The Three Little Pigs"
"Character Description" activity sheet (p. 35)
lined paper
pencils

Stimulus

1. Read the story "The Three Little Pigs" aloud to the class.
2. Discuss the characteristics of the three little pigs and of the wolf.
3. Then tell students the difference between physical traits and personality traits of a character. Explain that physical traits are those qualities that describe a character's outward appearance and that character traits (or personality traits) are those qualities that make up the nature of a character. Give examples of words to describe personality traits (examples might include "mean," "lazy," "smart," "happy-go-lucky," "cheerful").

Activity

1. Give each student a copy of the activity sheet. Conduct this activity with the entire class; if your students are capable of working in small groups, divide the class into groups of about five students each and have the groups work on their own to complete the activity sheet.
2. Have the students name traits for each pig and for the wolf, discuss the traits, and then list the traits in the correct column on the activity sheet.
3. Have each student write a short paragraph to sum up the physical and personality traits of one of the characters.

Follow-up

Have the students read their paragraphs aloud to the class.

Evaluation

Students may comment on each other's paragraphs as they are read. Reinforce the distinction between physical traits and personality traits by asking such questions as "If the character's mood changes, would that character still have the same physical traits?" A student may, for example, list "mean looking" as a physical trait; ask the class to tell how they know that the character looks mean (for example, "the wolf has long, sharp teeth"). Encourage students to use sensory words (sight, hearing, feel, or smell) when describing physical traits.

Variations

1. This activity works well with almost any folktale or fairy tale in which the characters have strong personalities. Try it with "Snow White and the Seven Dwarfs," "Rapunzel," or "Hansel and Gretel."
2. Read two stories to the class. Have students list the personality traits of one character from each story and then write a short paragraph to compare the characters.

Activity Sheet *Character Description*

Characters	Physical Traits	Personality Traits
pig 1		
pig 2		
pig 3		
wolf		

SAFE Lesson Plan — *Ask Me Again*

Objectives

Students will:
1. Complete a poem that contains a repeating pattern.
2. Discern rhythm in poetry.

Materials

Brown Bear, Brown Bear, What Do You See?, by Bill Martin, Jr.
"Ask Me Again" activity sheets (pp. 37–38)
lined paper
pencils

Stimulus

Read *Brown Bear, Brown Bear, What Do You See?* aloud to the class. After you read a few lines, the students will catch on to the pattern and will anticipate every other line. Encourage them to join in by saying these lines along with you as you read the lines. After you have read the story, call on students to continue the pattern, creating their own lines.

Activity

1. Give each student a copy of the activity sheet. This page contains the beginning of a poem pattern similar to the one in the book *Brown Bear, Brown Bear, What Do You See?*
2. Divide the class into groups of about four students each. The students in each group will work together to write at least six new "stanzas" of the poem. Students will follow the same format as that found in Bill Martin's book.
3. Each group may select a student to write their poem on lined paper first, as all the students in the group brainstorm new lines of the poem. Then the students may copy the poem onto their activity sheets.

Follow-up

Have the students illustrate their poems. Ask one student from each group to read the group's completed poem aloud to the class. Collect all of the illustrations and one copy of each poem to compile in a student booklet. Make the booklet available to other students in the school library.

Evaluation

Make sure all the students are contributing to the group poem. If it is practical, suggest that each student contribute two lines to the poem.

Variation

If your students need a challenge, distribute copies of the activity sheet on p. 38 instead. This activity requires more creativity and more advanced language skills, since students will be writing full lines and thinking of rhyming words. In addition, this worksheet requires students to use the past tense for verbs given in the present tense.

Activity Sheet *Ask Me Again*

Complete the poem. Use the pattern you see.

Little dog, little dog, what do you need?
I need a little squirrel that I can feed.

Little squirrel, little squirrel, what do you need?

Activity Sheet *Ask Me Again—Another Poem*

Use the words below to help you complete the questions. Underline the words that rhyme in each pair of lines.

Handy Sandy, what did you make?
"I made a boat to sail on the lake."

Handy Sandy, what did you find?
"I found a boy who is helpful and kind."

Handy Sandy, what did you _____?
"_____."

Handy Sandy, what did you _____?
"_____."

Handy Sandy, what did you _____?
"_____."

Activity Sheet *Picture This (continued)*

Write sentences for these pictures, too.

4.

5.

6.

41

Additional Writing Activities for Unit 3

Wordless Books
Collect several wordless books, such as *Look What I Can Do*, by Jose Aruego, *The Knitted Cat*, by Antonella Bolliger-Savelli, and *A Flying Saucer Full of Spaghetti*, by Fernando Krahn. Have the students work in pairs to choose a book and share their ideas as they "read" these books. Have the students create their own wordless books, drawing several pictures that relate an event. Help each student staple the pictures together in sequence to create a book.

Patterns in Books
Read Shel Silverstein's *The Giving Tree*, which offers a cumulative story pattern throughout the book. Have students tell stories of their own using this pattern. *Fortunately*, by Remy Charlip, is another book that you can use to stimulate students to write. Have students write sentences based on the pattern in this book. (Example: Fortunately, I caught a fish for dinner. Unfortunately, it was a shark and I almost became its dinner.)

Choral Reading
Enhance students' enjoyment of rhymes and the rhythm of language through choral reading. Write a poem or a song on the chalkboard. Read it aloud to the class. Then have the students repeat what you have read, listening to the flow of the language. Divide the class into small groups and have the students practice reading and interpreting the feel of the poem or song.

Book Covers
Have students make book covers for their favorite books. They may use large sheets of construction paper or sheets of heavy wrapping paper. Have students cut and paste designs for the covers or draw pictures that depict scenes from the book.

Mobiles
Divide the class into small groups and have the students in each group select a favorite story. The students will collect objects and draw pictures that relate to the story. Provide wire coat hangers, string, tape, wooden dowels, and other materials appropriate to mobile building. Allow the students to use their creativity, building their mobile together with the others in the group. Have each group present its mobile, explaining the significance of each object and picture. Then hang the mobiles around the classroom.

Exploring Shapes
Read *The Wing on a Flea: A Book About Shapes*, by Ed Emberly. Ask the students to search for triangular-shaped objects all around them, and to make a list (or draw pictures) of these objects. Have each student cut triangular holes in a sheet of construction paper to depict an object.

Unit 4

I Can Write!

Writing can be a difficult task. It requires a combination of abilities. As a teacher, you will have to support students' writing efforts through teaching strategies that remove obstacles to successful writing. Such strategies include prewriting activities, which help provide a sense of security for beginners. The four lesson plans in this chapter offer prewriting activities that may be used repeatedly and may be adapted to numerous writing lessons.

SAFE Lesson Plan *Words to Describe*

Objectives

Students will:
1. Cluster words that describe an object.
2. Write a sentence using one of the descriptive words.

Materials

a rabbit (a real one or a stuffed toy) or pictures of rabbits
"Words to Describe" activity sheet (p. 45)
"Clustering Diagram" activity sheet (p. 46)
pencils

Stimulus

1. Clustering is a prewriting technique that helps us generate and organize ideas. Write the main subject or idea (in this case, "rabbit") in the middle of the chalkboard. Then write associated words or phrases in circles attached to the main subject or idea, as shown in the example below.
2. Show the rabbit or the pictures of rabbits to the class. Make sure everyone has a chance to look closely at the rabbit or the pictures.
3. Then ask students to describe a rabbit. Ask "What does a rabbit *look* like? *Sound* like? *Feel* like? *Smell* like?" Write their responses in cluster form on the chalkboard. Have the class read the words and phrases aloud together.

Sample Cluster:

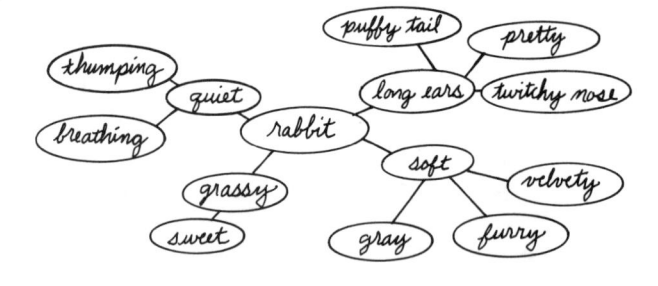

Activity

1. Give each student a copy of the activity sheet. Have students make their own clusters for a specific rabbit. Suggest that students use words listed on the chalkboard as well as others they think of.
2. Have each student write a sentence or two about the ideas in their cluster. More capable students may write a short paragraph.

Follow-up

1. Students may draw pictures to illustrate their sentences.
2. Have students read their sentences (or paragraphs) aloud to the class and then share their pictures.

Evaluation

Although the describing words need not be adjectives, they should help to describe or define the subject. Praise sentences and paragraphs that use the words in a meaningful way.

Variation

If you are sure that the students understand the activity, allow them to choose a different main subject, such as cat, dog, or horse, and use the activity sheet on p. 46. Students may use some of the same describing words and phrases listed on the chalkboard if they are appropriate. Choosing a new subject will help keep the activity fresh and creative, suggesting other adjectives.

Assign the clustering activity frequently as students prepare to write. Clustering helps students to generate ideas, to describe objects or topics, to observe detail, and to organize their thoughts. Clustering is an excellent approach to paragraph writing, since each cluster of words naturally forms the topic of a sentence in a paragraph.

Activity Sheet *Words to Describe*

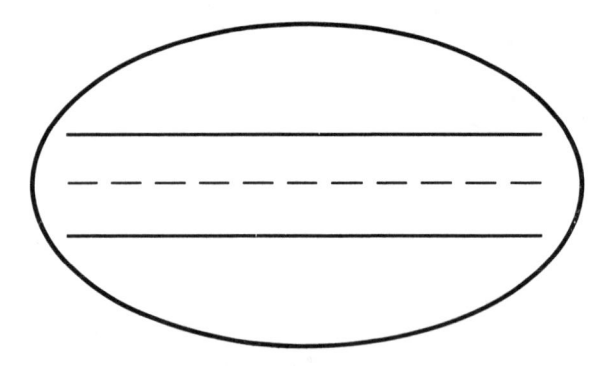

Activity Sheet *Clustering Diagram*

SAFE Lesson Plan

Making an Alphabet Book

Objectives

Students will:
1. List words that begin with each letter of the alphabet.
2. Write a sentence (or paragraph) about selected words.

Materials

children's alphabet books
butcher paper
tape
pencils
felt-tipped markers
"Making an Alphabet Book" activity sheet (p. 48)

Stimulus

Extend the stimulus portion of this lesson over a four-day period. Tape two or three lengths of butcher paper to the wall. Write the alphabet, spacing the letters far apart.

1. Read an alphabet book aloud to the class, or ask a student to read it aloud. Ask the students to name words that begin with *a*. List all of the words beside the letter *a* on the butcher paper chart. Use the same procedure for the letters *b* through *f*.
2. The following day, read another alphabet book to the class. Have students name words that begin with *g* through *l*, and list the words on the chart.
3. Continue the activity through two more days until there is a list of words on the chart for each letter of the alphabet.

Activity

1. Give each student a copy of the activity sheet. Assign each student a letter of the alphabet. If you have fewer than 26 students, assign two letters to some students; if you have more than 26 students, assign consonant blends and digraphs to some capable students. (Be sure to review blends and digraphs with the students.)
2. Ask each student to choose a word that represents her or his assigned letter. Students may choose a word from the chart or use a word that has not been listed.
3. Each student then completes the activity sheet, writing the assigned letter, the word he or she has chosen, and a sentence or short paragraph about the word. Students will then draw a picture on their activity sheets to illustrate the sentence or paragraph.

Follow-up

Collect the activity sheets. Have one or two students put them in alphabetical order; ask a couple of other students to check the pages. Bind the pages into a booklet, and make the booklet available for free-time reading.

Evaluation

Circulate through the classroom while the students are writing. Supply the correct spelling of key words representing the alphabet letters. As students read the booklet in their free time, they may comment on the use of unusual words or on interesting sentences and paragraphs.

Variation

Have each student draw a humorous self-portrait, first writing his or her initials on a blank sheet of paper and then incorporating the letters into a picture. Students will then write a sentence or paragraph explaining how the pictures portray their appearance or personality.

Activity Sheet *Making an Alphabet Book*

Letter: _____

Word: _____

SAFE Lesson Plan *Echoic Words*

Objectives

Students will:
1. Identify echoic words.
2. Write sentences using echoic words.

Materials

Umbrella, by Taro Yashima
tape recorder
"Echoic Words" activity sheet (p. 50)
lined paper
pencils

Stimulus

1. Explain that an echoic word is a word that sounds like what it means (for example, "buzz," "jingle," "chirp," or "thump").
2. Read *Umbrella* aloud to the class. Ask students to listen for echoic words. After you have read the story, have students name echoic words for you to list on the chalkboard.
3. Tape some real-life sounds (animal, mechanical, and instrumental sounds) on a tape recorder. Sounds that may be easy to record are a car engine, a lawn mower, a dog or cat, a computer printer, and a fly. Play the sounds for the class. Ask the students to identify the sounds and to create echoic words that imitate the sounds.

Activity

Give each student a copy of the activity sheet. Have students work on their own or in small groups to complete the assignment.

Follow-up

Have the students share their sentences with the class, reading them aloud or circulating them around the room for the others to read.

Evaluation

Praise the use of appropriate echoic words. For students' own sentences, comment on especially creative uses of echoic words, or on echoic words that the students have created themselves.

Variation

Have students pair up and, with their partners, compose paragraphs with echoic words. The partners will then read their paragraphs to the class, one student reading the regular words in each sentence and pausing at each echoic word to let the other student read the echoic word in an animated fashion.

Activity Sheet # Echoic Words

Here are some echoic words:

shriek	clank	chugged
plop	moo	hush
splash	whoosh	mutter
bang	slam	shhh
jingle	beep	slip

Read each sentence.
Write an echoic word in each blank.

1. The circus clown gave a _____ as the lion roared.

2. The trained seals made such a _____ when they jumped out of the water.

3. When the train _____ by, we heard the _____ of the bell.

On your own paper, write a story using other echoic words.

SAFE Lesson Plan — # Descriptive Phrases Chart

Objectives

Students will:
1. Retell a story in sequence.
2. Write descriptive words and phrases for the subject of a sentence.
3. Combine words and phrases to create meaningful sentences.

Materials

any popular folktale or fairy tale, such as "The Elves and the Shoemaker"
"Descriptive Phrases Chart" activity sheet (p. 52)
pencils
crayons

Stimulus

1. Read a folktale or fairy tale aloud to the class.
2. Choose a main character from the story. Write the name of that character on the chalkboard.
3. Ask students to name words that describe the main character. List these in a column on the chalkboard. Make sure all of these words are accurate and descriptive adjectives.
4. Ask students to recount the story's action, in sequence. As they speak, listen for the verb phrases they use to describe the story's action as it relates to the main character. List these verb phrases on the chalkboard.
5. With the students' help, choose a general noun that defines the character (examples: woman, boy, fairy, gremlin, troll). Write this noun between the two lists on the chalkboard.

```
Rumpelstiltskin
little            spun straw into gold
mean              wanted the queen's child
       man
old               stamped his foot
greedy            split in two
```

6. Review the lists, choosing one phrase from each column to complete a sentence. Call on students to create sentences similarly from the lists.

Activity

Give each student a copy of the activity sheet. Review the instructions and make sure everyone understands the assignment. Give the class about twenty minutes to complete the assignment on their own.

Follow-up

Have the students share their sentences with each other, reading them aloud to the class. Display the activity sheets on the bulletin board so that everyone may read them and may see the completed pictures.

Evaluation

Circulate around the classroom as the students are working. Check their lists. Make sure all the words they include in the first column are adjectives, and that the phrases they add to each of the other columns really belong in that column. Guide students who need help, offering verbs or prepositions to begin a phrase.

Variations

1. Younger students may wish to color the picture before they begin the activity. This will help them think of adjectives to describe the elf.
2. Capable students may compose a short paragraph about the elf in the illustration, using the sentence on the activity sheet as the opening sentence of the paragraph.

Activity Sheet # Descriptive Phrases Chart

Read the words in Column 1. They describe the elf above. Add two more words to describe the elf. Read the phrases in Columns 2 and 3. They describe action. Add two more phrases to each column.

Column 1 (describing)	Column 2 (action)	Column 3 (place)
tricky	asked for gold	on the beach
magic	made three wishes	at a friend's house
small	will make a wish	at the store

Choose words from each column to write a sentence about the elf. Write your sentence here.

_____
_____
_____

Complete the picture above to illustrate your sentence.

52

Additional Writing Activities for Unit 4

Hide the Star
Give each student a gummed star, a sheet of construction paper, and a sheet of lined paper. Ask students to imagine a picture that contains a star. Each student will stick the star anywhere on the construction paper and will draw a picture around it, using crayons or felt-tipped pens. After completing the picture, the student will write a sentence that begins to tell a story about the picture. Collect the papers and distribute them at random, making sure that no student has received her or his own papers. Ask each person to finish writing the story begun on the paper in hand. (Be sure to collect the pictures as well as the writing paper so that students will be able to add to the stories in a meaningful way.) Read the stories aloud, showing each accompanying picture.

Listing Poems
Direct students to write one word (such as "fox") on the first line of a sheet of writing paper. Each student will then pass her or his paper to the student on the right. That student will write two describing words on the next line and will pass the paper on. (These words should describe the word written on the first line.) The third person will write three action words on the next line and will pass the paper on once again. The fourth person will write four words that express a feeling, and will pass the paper on for the last time. The fifth person will write five words that ask a question and complete the poem. For example:

> Fox,
> Tiny, curious,
> Sniffing, whimpering, crouching,
> He is very unhappy.
> Where is his mother tonight?

Sound Poems
Make a sound with an object, such as rattling keys or closing a book. Ask the students to identify the sound. Then have them describe the sound, using metaphors and descriptive phrases. Write their phrases and sentences on the chalkboard. Then arrange the phrases and sentences into a free-verse poem. For example:

> Rattling keys.
> It sounds like
> Metal banging together,
> Petrified rocks,
> A windchime,
> Someone fiddling coins in a pocket.

Once students understand the procedure, they can work in small groups to write their own free-verse poems to describe other sounds.

Listening
Ask students to sit quietly for two minutes, closing their eyes and listening to the sounds around them. Afterwards, have them name the things they heard. List them on the chalkboard. Help the students arrange their phrases and sentences in a poem. For example, here is a poem entitled "Listen":

> The sound of quiet?
> Whispering voices,
> Wiggling bodies,
> Roaring lawn motors,
> Clickety-clack footsteps.

Rainbow Words
Make one copy of p. 54 for each student. Have the students color the page using crayons or felt-tipped pens and decorate the page as they wish. This piece of art may serve as a poster or perhaps as the cover for a student-made book. Talk about the meaning of the expression "Bright is the rainbow of words."

Bright is the rainbow of words

Learning to Use Written Language © 1987, David S. Lake Publishers

Unit 5

Getting into Narrative Writing

As students read or listen to more stories, they become increasingly aware of basic writing formats and writing techniques. Most primary students can tell the difference between poetry and prose, and between realistic fiction and fantasy fiction. Many primary students can sense the difference betwen a fable, a fairy tale or folktale, and other types of stories. Students may even be able to write a short story of an assigned type.

As students are exposed to more writing, they learn that a story can be told from different perspectives. As students' language skills improve and they learn how to use quotation marks, they will understand how dialogue works. This unit contains lessons for students who are really getting into creative writing! Although these lessons may seem more sophisticated than lessons in earlier units, they are still appropriate for use in primary classrooms.

SAFE Lesson Plan # Happiness Is . . .

Objectives

Students will:
1. Use metaphors to express an abstract idea.
2. Expand a one-sentence expression into a paragraph.

Materials

Happiness Is a Warm Puppy, by Charles Schulz
lined paper
pencils

Stimulus

Read the book *Happiness Is a Warm Puppy* aloud to the class. Write the phrase "Happiness is . . ." on the chalkboard. Then ask the students what happiness is to them. (Give them a minute or so to collect their thoughts before they answer.) Direct their responses to suggest what represents happiness or what creates a happy feeling for each of them. Each response is actually a metaphor for the word "happiness."

Activity

Give each student a sheet of lined paper. Ask the students to complete the sentence "Happiness is . . ." writing their responses to the question you posed earlier. Have each student write a short paragraph to explain why that item represents happiness.

Follow-up

Have the students illustrate their paragraphs. Then ask them to read their paragraphs aloud to each other in groups of four. Each group can choose one paragraph to share with the class.

Evaluation

Make sure that students complete the sentence "Happiness is . . ." with a metaphor and complete a short paragraph. Display the selected paragraphs on a bulletin board.

SAFE Lesson Plan — *Teddy Bear Picnic*

Objectives

Students will:
1. Name words to describe their teddy bears.
2. Imagine and tell about activities and adventures that teddy bears might enjoy at a picnic.
3. Write a story about a picnic for teddy bears.

Materials

Anne Murray's recording of "The Teddy Bear Picnic"
blankets
picnic-type snacks
paper plates and napkins
a few teddy bears
"Teddy Bear Picnic" activity sheet (p. 58)
pencils

Stimulus

Plan a teddy bear picnic a week in advance. Send a letter home to students' parents stating the date, the time, and the purpose of the picnic. Request that students bring their own teddy bears to class on that day. Those students who do not bring teddy bears can "adopt" one from you, if you bring enough extras.

1. Play the Anne Murray recording of "The Teddy Bear Picnic." Encourage the students to listen carefully to the words. Discuss the song with the class.
2. Divide the class into groups of four students each. Spread blankets on the floor around the classroom and have the groups of students sit on blankets for their picnic. Serve the snack while "The Teddy Bear Picnic" plays softly in the background. When students have finished their snacks, have them help clean up, fold the blankets and put them away, and then return to their desks.

Activity

1. Ask students to describe their teddy bears. List on the chalkboard the descriptive words they mention. Then ask them to imagine what activities or adventures teddy bears might enjoy at a picnic. As they offer ideas, write them on the chalkboard.
2. Give each student a copy of the activity sheet. (Make several extra copies.) Have each student compose a story about a teddy bear's picnic, writing the story on the activity sheet. Students may use their own ideas or those listed on the chalkboard. They may continue their stories on extra copies of the activity sheet if necessary.

Follow-up

Have students read their stories to the class. Display the completed stories on a bulletin board.

Evaluation

Discuss the activity with the class. Ask them to name new words and ideas they learned as a result of the activity. Have them tell what they liked and what they disliked about the lesson.

Activity Sheet *Teddy Bear Picnic*

Write a story about a teddy bear's picnic.

SAFE Lesson Plan # *From Fear to Story*

Objectives

Students will:
1. Write a paragraph to describe an actual fear.
2. Collectively write a creative story about how one fear is overcome.

Materials

There's a Nightmare in My Closet, by Mercer Mayer
"From Fear to Story" activity sheet (p. 60)
"From Fear to Story" student example (p. 61)
lined paper
pencils

Stimulus

Read the book *There's a Nightmare in My Closet* aloud to the class. Summarize the story; explain that the story tells how a young boy overcomes his fear of nightmares. Discuss the story with the class. Ask the following questions to generate discussion:
- What was the little boy afraid of?
- What did he do to avoid the nightmare?
- What did the nightmare look like?
- Do you think the boy is still afraid of nightmares?
- Which parts of the story could actually happen?
- Which parts of the story could not happen in real life?

Activity

1. Ask students to think about fears they experienced when they were younger, or even fears they still have.
2. Give each student a copy of the activity sheet. Have students jot down three or four fears. Then allow about ten minutes for the students to write a short paragraph about one of the fears. Suggest one of the following beginnings to the paragraph: "When I was young, I was afraid of . . ." or "Even now, I am sometimes a little afraid of . . ." Make sure students address the questions listed on the activity sheet.
3. Divide the class into small groups. Have the students in each group read their paragraphs to each other and choose one paragraph to expand into a story.
4. Give each student a copy of the student sample (p. 61), and have the students take turns reading it aloud. This page provides an example of the type of story the students will be writing.
5. Give each group a few sheets of lined paper. Have them collectively write a story (about four paragraphs) based on the student-written paragraph they selected. The story may be fictionalized or it may simply be an expansion of the original paragraph. The focus of the story should be overcoming the fear.

Follow-up

1. Ask one student in each group to read the story. After each story is read, discuss how the fear was overcome. Ask students whether the events are realistic or fantastic, and if they have other suggestions for overcoming such a fear.
2. Bind the stories in a class book and make it available for free-time reading.

Evaluation

Observe class participation during the story writing. Collect the activity sheets, comment on the students' paragraphs (consider how well the students address the questions listed on the activity sheet), and return the paragraphs to the students.

Activity Sheet *From Fear to Story*

Tell about a fear you have now or had when you were younger.
Write a paragraph that tells about the fear.
Think about these questions. Answer them in your paragraph.

- What caused the fear?
- When did you feel afraid?
- What did you do when you felt afraid?
- Did you try to avoid the fear? If so, how?
- Did you overcome the fear? If so, how?

Student Example *From Fear to Story*

When I was young, I was afraid of horses. My older brother loved horses. I was afraid that my brother's horse, Rusty, would hurt me. Rusty is very big. Sometimes he bumps into me. I think he does it on purpose.

One night I went to bed early. I was just about to fall asleep. Then, a little horse with sparkly wings pranced into my room. He was beautiful. The horse said, "Come with me. I am a magical flying horse. Do not be afraid." I climbed on the horse's back and we flew away together over the treetops. Before long, we landed at a charming place. There were other horses there. I spoke to them gently. I brushed the horses. I learned how to ride them. Then the magical flying horse flew me home.

The next day, I ran outside to see Rusty. I talked to him gently, and I brushed him. I was no longer afraid.

SAFE Lesson Plan *Taking Another Point of View*

Objectives

Students will:
1. Identify point of view in a story.
2. Rewrite the story from another point of view.

Materials

Alexander and the Terrible, Horrible, No Good, Very Bad Day, by Judith Viorst (or any other story told from the first person)
lined paper
pencils

Stimulus

1. Read *Alexander and the Terrible, Horrible, No Good, Very Bad Day* aloud to the class. (You may substitute any other story told from the first person.) Discuss the story with the class. Ask the students to identify the character telling the story (Alexander). Then ask them to name some personality traits of this character. Name some other characters (such as Anthony or Alexander's mother) and have the students suggest personality traits of these characters (there are no right answers).
2. Explain "point of view" as a way of looking at something. Explain that all stories are told from someone's point of view, and that sometimes the story is told from the point of view of a character in the story. Many times, however, the story is not told by one of the characters.
3. Summarize Alexander's character again, and lead students to tell how the story is influenced by his character.

Activity

Give each student a sheet of lined paper. Have the students choose another point of view from which to tell Alexander's story. Suggest they tell the story from Anthony's point of view or from Alexander's mother's point of view. The students may even tell the story from their own point of view.

Follow-up

Have each student read his or her story aloud to the class. Ask the students to identify the point of view from which the student's story is told.

Evaluation

Make sure that the point of view is consistent throughout each student's story. Praise stories that offer a new angle along with the new point of view.

Variation

Give each student a copy of the "Mini-Book Publications" blackline master (p. 63). Students will write one paragraph on each quarter page to complete a story. Direct students to fold the page along the broken lines to construct a small booklet. Duplicate this form for numerous applications.

Mini-Book Publications

Title: _____

By: _____

Place: _____

Date: _____

Page 2

Once upon a time _____

Page 3

The very next day _____

Page 4

At last _____

Additional Writing Activities for Unit 5

Point of View

Have the students rewrite a familiar folktale or fairy tale from another character's point of view. Have the students work in small groups, each person taking a different point of view for the same story. Group members can then compare their stories from their different perspectives. Point out how the story changes with a different point of view, even though the plot remains the same.

Changing Times

Have the students rewrite a familiar folktale or fairy tale to suit another time period. The students would have to adjust the lifestyles of the characters as well as the language. For example:

> Little Red Ridinghood was speeding through the woods on her motorcycle when it suddenly stalled and refused to budge. Along came the wolf in his blue convertible Cad. "Hey, Little Red," he called out.

Students can work in small groups or on their own to write their stories.

Descriptive Paragraphs

Ask each student to describe an object, in writing, without identifying the object. Have the students read their paragraphs aloud and have the rest of the class try to guess the object. If no one can guess the object, the student must tell what it is. Then ask the class to name words they might use to describe the object.

Personal Narrative

Begin narrating a few memorable experiences you would like to relate to the class. Examples:

> I remember going on a hayride in a big wagon.
> I remember a cold rainy day when the mail carrier brought a big package.

Give the students a few minutes to think of some memorable experiences. Then ask each student to write an "I remember" statement for at least three experiences. The statement can identify the event, or the student can use the statement to indicate the emotion of the experience. Examples:

> I remember laughing so hard I cried.
> I remember being really, really scared.
> I remember going down a steep hill on a sled.
> I remember catching my first fish.
> I remember my pet turtle named Snoopy.

Divide the class into small groups and have each student read one of the statements and complete the story orally. Then have the students write the stories they told.

Unit 6

Expository Writing

Expository writing is the act of explaining, using written words. It takes many different forms—essays, letters, articles, and so on. Expository writing requires higher-level thinking skills because it demands logical, organized paragraph development. This may sound pretty advanced, but, in fact, even primary students benefit from simple expository writing exercises.

This unit contains lessons that help primary students learn to recognize various forms of expository writing, organize a paragraph, and expand a topic sentence into a paragraph. These lessons challenge students' logical thinking skills. Perhaps most important, students will learn that the purpose of writing is to communicate a thought or an idea.

How to Organize a Paragraph

- He loves to sit on my shoulder.
- He does not mean to scare people.
- My hamster is the friendliest creature.
- He eats out of my hand.
- My hamster is a great pet.

SAFE Lesson Plan *Letter Writing*

Objectives

Students will write a three-part letter.

Materials

"Letter Writing" example (p. 67)
overhead projector
"Letter Writing" activity sheet
 (p. 68)
pencils

Stimulus

1. A couple of weeks before you begin this activity, contact a teacher from another school—perhaps one in a different city or state—who may be interested in having her or his students write letters to your students.
2. Make a copy of the letter writing example. Fill in the blanks on this copy as if you have written this letter yourself. Then make a transparency of your letter. Show the letter to your class, by using an overhead projector and displaying it on a screen. Point out the three parts to a letter—the greeting, the body of the letter, and the closing. Ask a few students to take turns reading the letter aloud to the class.
3. Tell the class what a pen pal is. Ask if anyone has a pen pal. If you have found a class of students who would like to correspond with your students, discuss how this arrangement will work as you exchange letters.

Activity

1. Give each student a copy of the letter writing example and a copy of the activity sheet.
2. Have each student write a letter on the activity sheet form. Be sure they write a greeting and a closing and at least one paragraph in the body of the letter. (Also suggest that they date their letters.) Students may use the example as a model. Suggest that they write a rough draft of their letters on the back of the example page before writing the final letter on the activity sheet. Encourage students to write original sentences according to their abilities.

Follow-up

1. Have students pair off and exchange letters. Each should read the other's letter and make suggestions for improving it.
2. Students can revise and rewrite their letters in final form for mailing.

Evaluation

Each student will read her or his partner's letter and comment on it. Students should check that the letter contains a greeting, a closing, and at least one paragraph in the body. Students may help each other with spelling, punctuation, and word use.

If you have arranged for pen pals, collect the letters, read them, and send them to the teacher with whom you made arrangements.

Example *Letter Writing*

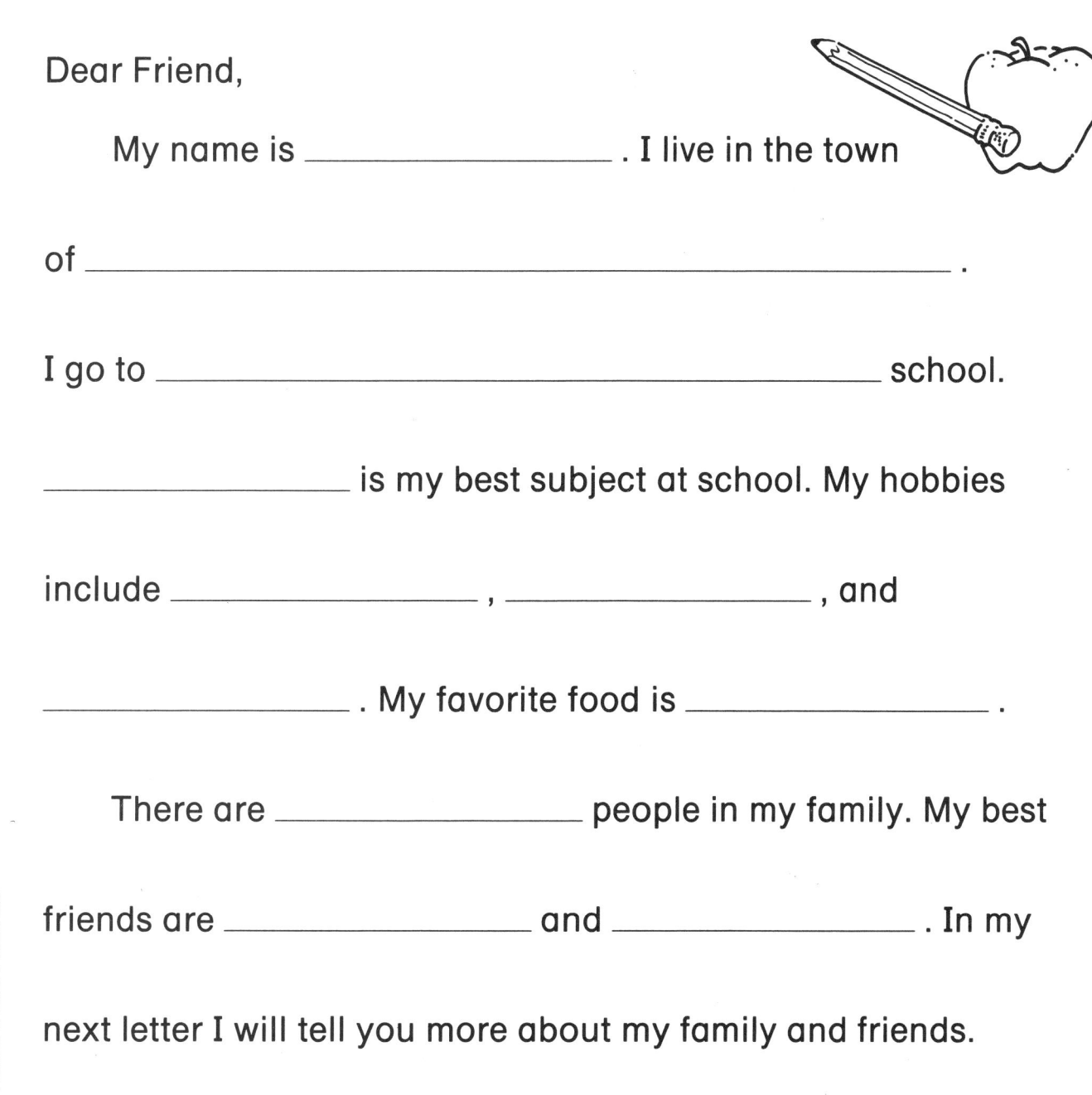

Dear Friend,

My name is _____ . I live in the town

of _____ .

I go to _____ school.

_____ is my best subject at school. My hobbies

include _____ , _____ , and

_____ . My favorite food is _____ .

There are _____ people in my family. My best

friends are _____ and _____ . In my

next letter I will tell you more about my family and friends.

Please write back and tell me about yourself.

Your pen pal,

_____

67

Activity Sheet *Letter Writing*

SAFE Lesson Plan — *Mapping a Paragraph*

Objectives

Students will:
1. Organize information into a paragraph.
2. Write a paragraph with a topic sentence, supporting sentences, and a concluding sentence.

Materials

"Mapping a Paragraph" activity sheet (p. 70)
"Paragraph Worksheet" activity sheet (p. 71)
pencils

Stimulus

1. Mapping is a way of organizing information visually. Explain that a paragraph is a series of sentences that tell about one subject or idea. In the mapping activity that follows, a paragraph will contain a topic sentence, at least three supporting sentences, and a concluding statement.
2. Draw a mapping diagram on the chalkboard. (See the one below.)
3. Choose a subject or idea for your example. Write a topic sentence in the oval at the center of the mapping diagram. The topic sentence should identify your main subject or idea.
4. Ask questions about the main subject to generate supporting sentences. For example, if the topic sentence is "Friends are important," ask why friends are important, or what activities involve friends, or if anyone has needed a friend during an emergency. Write each supporting sentence on a line that radiates from the center oval.

Activity

1. Brainstorm paragraph topics with the class. Write at least ten subjects or ideas (such as toys, books, animals, sports, or abstract ideas such as happiness or fear) on the chalkboard.
2. Give each student a copy of the activity sheet. Have each student choose a topic and complete a mapping diagram for that topic. Allow about 30 minutes for this activity.
3. Give each student a copy of the paragraph worksheet. Direct students to fill in the worksheet, writing each complete sentence that the paragraph would contain, in order, based on the mapping diagram.

Follow-up

Have students pair up and exchange mapping diagrams and paragraph worksheets with a partner. Students will then read each other's diagrams and worksheets.

Evaluation

Students should compare the diagram and worksheets to make sure the sentences on the worksheet reflect the notes on the diagrams. Remind students that the topic sentence should identify the subject or idea of the paragraph, that there should be at least three supporting sentences that give further detail, and that the concluding sentence should express about the same thing as the topic sentence. Collect the papers and read those paragraphs (reading from the worksheets) that have the most logical organized construction.

Activity Sheet *Mapping a Paragraph*

Write your topic sentence in the center.
On each line, write a sentence that gives detail.
At the bottom, write a sentence to sum up your idea.

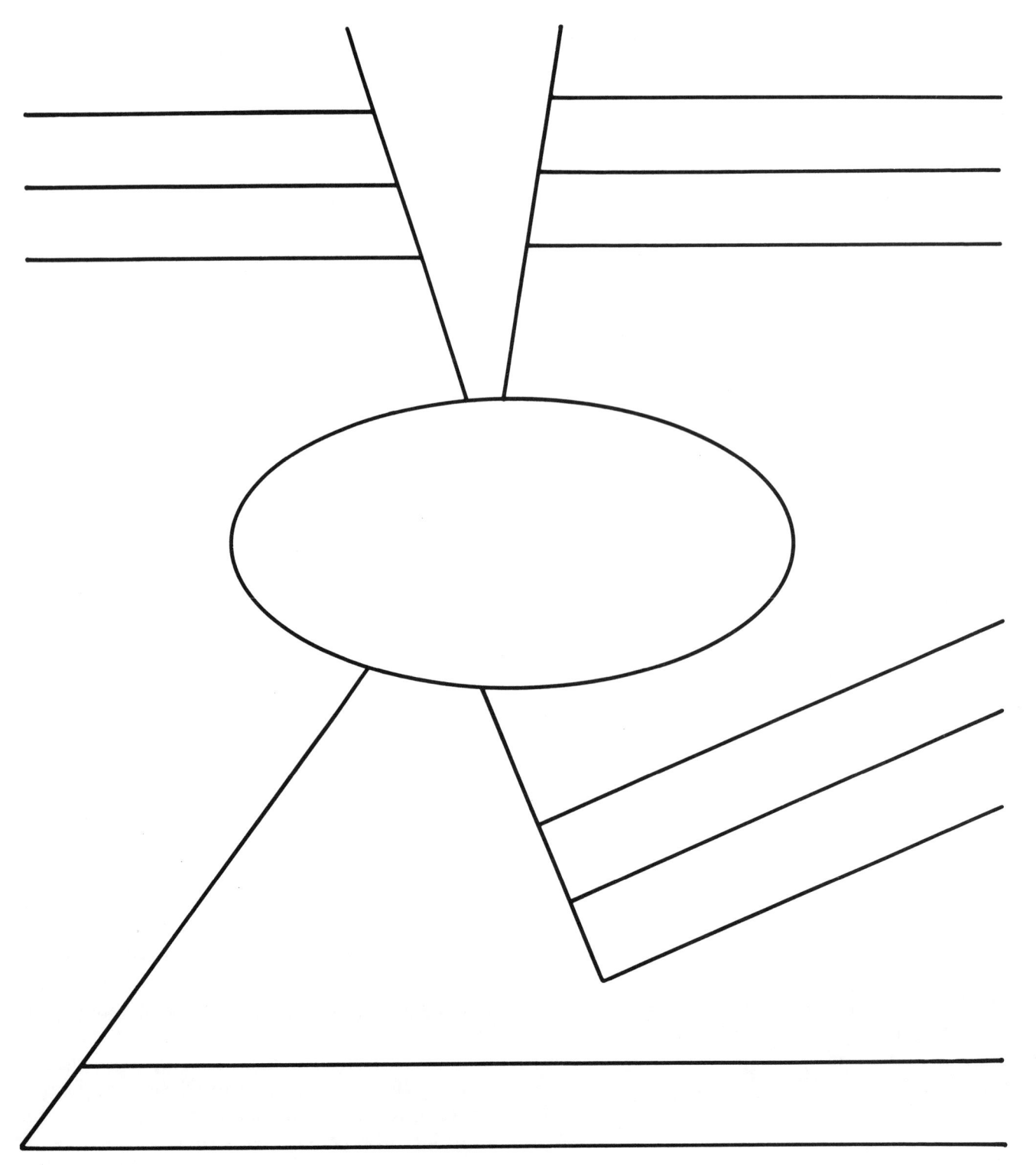

Activity Sheet *Paragraph Worksheet*

Write the paragraph you mapped out.
Write each sentence on the correct line.
Read the sentences in order. Does your paragraph make sense?

Main topic or idea:	
Supporting sentences: (Each sentence gives detail about your main topic or idea.)	
Concluding statement: (The sentence restates your main topic or idea in a different way.)	

SAFE Lesson Plan *Grocery Shopping*

Objectives

Students will:
1. Identify the function of each sentence in a paragraph.
2. Write an expository paragraph about a shopping experience.

Materials

grocery bag full of items
"Grocery Shopping" activity sheet (p. 73)
pencils

Stimulus

1. Fill a grocery bag with items such as fresh produce, canned goods, paper goods, and so on. To represent perishable items such as milk or frozen meat pies, include the empty cartons or boxes.
2. Bring the bag to class. Place it on a table in front of the class. Call on students to come up to the front of the class, one at a time, and remove one item from the bag. All of the students will name the item, and the student holding the item will list it on the chalkboard.
3. Write the following paragraph (or a similar paragraph) on the chalkboard:

Last week my father and I went shopping at our favorite supermarket. We bought steaks and fish in the meat section. In the produce section we bought potatoes, peaches, and oranges. We also bought bread and milk. My parents like to shop at the supermarket.

Ask one student to read the paragraph aloud. Call on another student to label each sentence 1 (topic sentence), 2 (supporting statements), or 3 (concluding statement). Ask the other students to confirm the labeling.

Activity

Give each student a copy of the activity sheet. Have students write an expository paragraph about an experience they have had grocery shopping with a parent. Each paragraph must contain a topic sentence, at least three supporting or detail sentences, and a concluding statement.

Follow-up

1. Have students color the picture on the activity sheet and draw grocery items around the page.
2. Divide the class into groups of about five students. Each student will read her or his paragraph to the group. The other students in the group will note whether the paragraph contains a topic sentence, supporting sentences, and a concluding sentence.
3. Collect the paragraphs and bind them in a book entitled "We Go Grocery Shopping."

Evaluation

The students will be evaluating each other's paragraphs in their small groups. After you have collected the paragraphs, choose a few that particularly exemplify the paragraph criteria. Read these aloud, praise the authors, and explain why you have chosen these paragraphs.

Variation

Have students write on other topics such as "Shopping at the Hardware Store" or "A Visit to the Dentist."

Activity Sheet *Grocery Shopping*

Think about an experience you had grocery shopping. Write a paragraph about this experience.

SAFE Lesson Plan *Snail Articles*

Objectives

Students will:
1. In writing, tell facts about garden snails.
2. Write an article about snails using a prescribed format.

Materials

jar of real snails
black construction paper
children's book about snails
"Snail Articles" activity sheet (p. 75)
lined paper
pencils
crayons

Stimulus

1. The night before this lesson, collect about ten live garden snails and place them in a jar with air holes. (See the variation below.)
2. Divide the class into small groups. Give one snail and one sheet of black paper to each group.
3. Direct the students to place the snail on the paper and watch it move. The snail's trail will be apparent on the black paper.

Activity

1. Give each student a copy of the activity sheet. Have students complete the page, writing at least one sentence for each heading. Students may tell facts (in writing) based on their observations, or they may find information in the snail books.
2. Give each student a sheet of lined paper. Each student will organize his or her sentences into an article, write the article on lined paper, and illustrate the article.

Follow-up

Ask students to volunteer to read their articles aloud to the class. Collect the articles and read all of them. Bind the articles in a book, and make it available for the students to read during free time.

Evaluation

Praise articles that are logical, well-organized, and informative. Also commend those articles that are especially inventive or creative.

Variation

Conduct the following art lesson as an alternative to bringing live snails to class. Have each student make a snail shell by decorating the back of a small dessert-type paper plate, using felt-tipped pens, so the plate looks like a real snail shell. The student then will glue the plate onto a sheet of light-colored construction paper and will draw the snail's body and scenery around the snail. Students may instead color and glue dry shell-type macaroni onto the paper plate to texture the snail shell.

Use this art lesson as a stimulus to a creative writing lesson about snails. Have students write adventure stories told from a snail's point of view.

Activity Sheet *Snail Articles*

See what you can learn about snails.
Write at least one sentence for each heading.

What a snail looks like:

How a snail moves:

Where you could find a snail:

What snails eat:

75

Additional Writing Activities for Unit 6

I Believe
Have each student write five statements of opinion that begin "I believe." Examples:
 I believe that people like the color red best.
 I believe I will get a bicycle for my next birthday.

Then have the students choose one of their statements to write a paragraph about, adding three sentences to explain why they have that belief.

A Horrible Day
Read Judith Viorst's *Alexander and the Terrible, Horrible, No Good, Very Bad Day* to the class. Ask the students to help you list all the terrible things that happened to Alexander. Write the key words on the chalkboard. After listing these things, dictate the following sentence and have the students copy it on lined paper: "Alexander had a terrible, horrible, no good, very bad day." Direct the students to write three sentences telling some of the things that happened to Alexander, and a final sentence summing up the paragraph. Each student probably will have written a well-constructed expository paragraph.

Categories
Write a word on the chalkboard that most students can identify with, such as "bear," or "playground." Ask what word comes to mind when they hear that word. List their responses on the chalkboard. Then ask what words in the list go together. As specific categories emerge, write the category headings on the chalkboard and number them. Then number each word accordingly. Have students write sentences using the words from specified categories.

How-To Explanation
Have students write a paragraph explaining a step-by-step procedure, such as how to make lemonade, how to put on a shirt, or how to tie shoelaces. Ask the students to share their paragraphs with the class. As each student reads the paragraph aloud, have another student follow the directions to demonstrate the procedure.

Reporting
Arrange for a surprise incident to take place in the classroom. Make sure the scene will be witnessed by all of your students. For example, you might arrange for a student from another class to run into your classroom and take several books from your desk while you are preoccupied teaching. Have each student write an account of the incident. Then divide the class into small groups and have the students discuss the incident, comparing their accounts. Ask several students to reenact the scene; try to arrive at a consensus.

Unit 7

Editing Your Writing

Editing is an important part of the writing task. Primary students often merely recopy their compositions for neatness, neglecting to consider the mechanics of writing—spelling, punctuation, and grammar—or the more style-related matters such as wording, sentence variety, and tone. It is difficult for students to think of writing in stages. Writing a composition is sometimes so difficult for students that they cannot imagine having to *rewrite* the same composition! A first draft, though, can almost always be improved by editing and revising. The more practice students have with editing, the easier it will be for them to accept the "stages" approach to writing.

The first two lessons in this unit focus on the mechanics of writing. These other lessons are a good way to ease students into editing. Three other lessons help students edit for vocabulary, clarity, detail, and interest. Students will be editing their own work as well as each other's writing. As students grow accustomed to editing, they will learn for themselves about the qualities of effective composition.

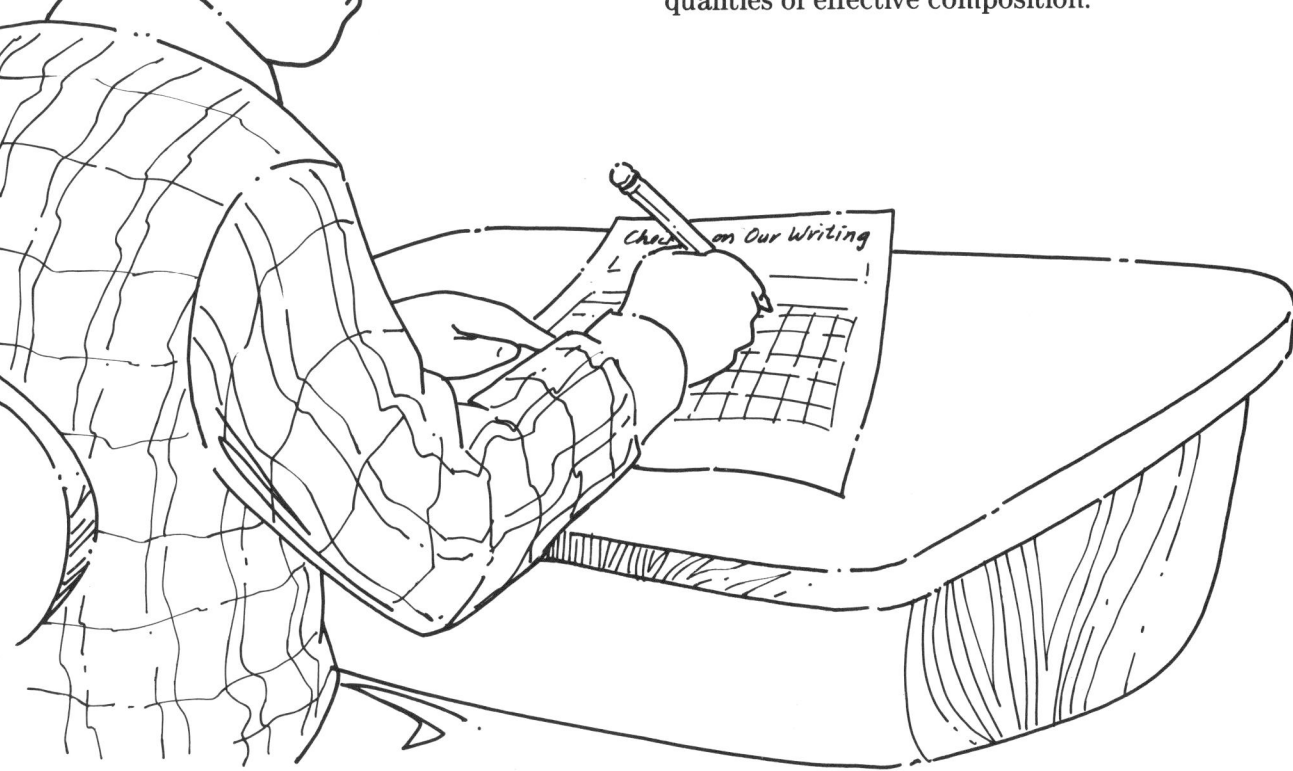

SAFE Lesson Plan — *Capital Letters*

Objectives

Students will use the correct capitalization for:
1. The first word in a sentence.
2. Names.
3. The days of the week, months, and holidays.
4. The pronoun *I*.

Materials

index cards
felt-tipped pens
"Capital Letters" activity sheet (p. 79)
pencils

Stimulus

1. Have each student write "capital letter" on an index card.
2. Read a sentence aloud to the class. Read it again slowly, each word at a time. Have students hold up their cards when they hear a word that should begin with a capital letter. Read about ten different sentences, all of which need only the first word capitalized. (With the example "Jeremy ran to the store," students will hold up their cards when they hear the word "Jeremy.")
3. At random, ask the students why they flashed their cards. Students should state the word that should be capitalized and the reason why.
4. Write the same sentences, without capitalization, on the chalkboard. Have students copy the sentences on paper, correcting the capitalization.
5. Repeat this procedure over the course of a few days, working on one capitalization objective at a time. The sentences you read aloud and write on the chalkboard should reflect the objective (names, days of the week, months, holidays, and the pronoun *I*).

Activity

Give each student a copy of the activity sheet. Have students work independently to rewrite the sentences, correcting the capitalization. You may wish to assign this activity sheet as homework.

Follow-up

Have students pair up and, individually, write sentences without any capital letters. Partners will then exchange papers and rewrite each sentence, correcting the capitalization.

Evaluation

Collect the completed activity sheets and grade them. Display all the papers that are 85% correct. (Each capital letter scores five points.) Work with the students who achieved lower scores.

Activity Sheet *Capital Letters*

Rewrite each sentence with the correct capitalization.

1. he will go to canada.

2. mrs. brown bought a puppy.

3. i saw sue on thursday.

4. it is warm in september.

5. my friend and i like halloween.

6. may i ask my grandmother?

7. she has a cat named whiskers.

8. where are tom and dan?

SAFE Lesson Plan *Punctuation*

Objectives

Students will:
1. Write a variety of sentences—telling, asking, and exclamatory.
2. Unscramble words to create meaningful sentences.
3. Use the correct punctuation at the end of a sentence.

Materials

index cards
felt-tipped pens
lined paper
pencils

Stimulus

1. Have each student make a set of punctuation cards—one card having a period, one having a question mark, and one having an exclamation point.
2. Dictate sentences, one at a time, to the class. Use a variety of telling, asking, and exclamatory sentences.
3. Have the class hold up the correct index card to show the correct end-of-line punctuation for each sentence.

Activity

1. Divide the class into groups of about six students.
2. Have each group collectively write three sentences—one telling, one asking, and one exclamatory.
3. Have the students in each group write their sentences on the chalkboard, scrambling the word order in each sentence and omitting the end-of-line punctuation.
4. Challenge the other students in the class to unscramble each sentence and write it correctly, with the correct end-of-line punctuation, on lined paper.

Follow-up

Duplicate a passage from the students' reading text. White out the punctuation mark at the end of each sentence. Make a copy of this page for each student, and challenge the students to write the correct punctuation mark in each place.

Evaluation

Observe student participation during the stimulus portion of this lesson. Students who are hesitant about the index card they hold up probably need more practice with punctuation. Appoint two students to serve as editors to check student papers against the original text as each one finishes. Students who make errors should check their sentences against the text and make corrections.

Variation

If your students have a good understanding of commas and quotation marks, have each student make an index card for each of these marks. Dictate sentences that require them to flash cards showing commas, quotation marks, periods, question marks, and exclamation points.

SAFE Lesson Plan *My Own Personal Dictionary*

Objectives

Students will:
1. Keep a record of words they frequently misspell or misuse.
2. Refer to their personal dictionary when editing.

Materials

small three-ring binder
lined paper to fit the binders
pencils

Stimulus

Have a class spelling bee using words from the students' vocabulary lists or textbooks. Use words from a variety of subject areas so that students realize it is important to spell and use words correctly in all academic areas, not just in language arts. Try a "word use bee": have the student give a definition or an example for a word after spelling it.

Activity

The students should purchase their own three-ring binders and paper. Each student will begin by adding 26 sheets of lined paper to her or his binder, labeling each page with a letter of the alphabet. Choose about ten words that students frequently misspell (such as *friend, surprise, second, eight, canoe, half, once, enough, break,* and *monkeys*) or misuse (such as most homonyms—*there* and *their, here* and *hear*). Have the students list each of these words in their dictionaries, on the correct page, and give a brief definition of the word.

Follow-up

1. As students are revising their compositions, they should make a dictionary entry for any word they misspelled or misused, writing the correct spelling and a brief definition of the word. Students should make a check mark beside any word they still seem to misspell or misuse frequently.
2. Display the dictionaries during Open House.

Evaluation

Check periodically to make sure students are making entries in their personal dictionaries and are referring to the dictionaries as they proofread and revise their compositions.

SAFE Lesson Plan — *Expanding Sentences*

Objectives

Students will:
1. Expand simple sentences by adding detail.
2. Rewrite a paragraph, adding descriptive detail.

Materials

"Expanding Sentences" activity sheet (p. 83)
pencils

Stimulus

Ask students to generate two-word sentences that begin with the name of a person. Examples:

Molly dances.
Abu played.
Carlos ran.

Write the sentences on the chalkboard. Choose one of the sentences to expand. Ask students to suggest ideas that add interest to the sentence and tell more exactly what is happening. For example:

On Monday afternoon, Carlos ran home as fast as he could because his mother had a surprise for him.

Emphasize the reason for expanding the sentences: the added words explain the action and provide the time and place of the action. The meaning is clearer in the expanded sentence than in the original sentence.

Activity

Give each student a copy of the activity sheet. Read the directions aloud, and make sure the students understand the activity. Show students how to use the caret symbol to make word insertions. At this point, students should simply add words to provide detail, rather than changing existing words. Allow about twenty minutes for students to edit the sentences.

Follow-up

After students have completed the writing activity, ask them to count the words they added to each sentence. Have students write the total number of added words at the top of the activity sheet. Discuss various ways to expand the sentences, and call on students to read their expanded sentences.

Evaluation

Have students pair up and read each other's revised sentences. Partners should check the mechanics in the sentences. They might challenge whether certain additions clarify meaning or make the story more interesting.

Ways to Extend This Activity

Discuss possible ways of rewriting the sentences, substituting more precise or more descriptive words for those in the paragraph (for example, substituting "terrier" or "mutt" for "dog"). Have students rewrite the paragraph, adding and substituting words as they wish.

Activity Sheet *Expanding Sentences*

You are the editor of a magazine. You want to publish this paragraph, but it is not very interesting. Your job is to add words that:

1. Make the meaning clear.
2. Make the paragraph more interesting.

   A boy saw a dog on the street. The dog was thin. The boy ran to the dog. The dog wagged its tail. The boy said, "I will take you home." The boy and the dog walked home. They became friends.

Now add words to make each sentence more interesting.

A boy saw a dog on the street.

The dog was thin.

The boy ran to the dog.

The dog wagged its tail.

The boy said, "I will take you home."

The boy and the dog walked home.

They became friends.

SAFE Lesson Plan

Checking on Our Writing

Objectives

Students will:
1. Identify the characteristics of a fable.
2. Write a fable.
3. Evaluate each other's writing according to a checklist.

Materials

Fables, by Arnold Lobel
"Checking on Our Writing" activity sheet (p. 85)
lined paper
pencils

Stimulus

Read two fables from Arnold Lobel's book aloud to the class. Discuss the characteristics of a fable. (A fable always has a moral, or a lesson, which is usually presented at the end of the story.)

Activity

1. Give each student a copy of the activity sheet. Although students will not be using this page until the follow-up activity, it lists characteristics of a fable and may be a useful reference during the writing activity.
2. Have students brainstorm proverbs to use as morals for fables. Here are some examples.

    A stitch in time saves nine.
    Don't cry over spilt milk.
    Look before you leap.

3. Give each student a sheet of lined paper. Have each student choose a proverb and write an original fable that ends with a moral based on the chosen proverb.

Follow-up

Divide the class into groups of four or five students. Read the directions on the activity sheet with the students, and make sure they understand the assignment. Have students share their fables with the group members and fill out the activity sheet, commenting on the student-written fables. Each student may read his or her story aloud, or students may pass around their stories and read them silently.

Evaluation

Students are evaluating each other's (and their own) writing in small groups. Circulate around the classroom and note how the editing process is working out.

Activity Sheet *Checking on Our Writing*

A good fable teaches a lesson, tells a story about the lesson, and is interesting.

Write the name of each group member. Take turns reading your fables. Give a score for each fable. Score on five items. For each item, give a score of 1, 2, or 3. The best score is 3. Then total the scores. The best total score is 15.

Group Member

Item:					
1. The lesson, or moral, of the fable					
2. The beginning of the story					
3. The middle of the story					
4. The end of the story					
5. The description in the story					
TOTAL SCORE					

In your group, talk about the scores. Agree on the scores together.

85

Additional Writing Activities for Unit 7

Read It Aloud
The first thing students should do to check a composition they have written is to read it aloud to themselves. As they read, they should listen for how the sentences sound. By testing their writing against their "ear for language," they will notice whether sentences are awkward or choppy. Suggest that students read each other's work aloud as they begin editing. Because we tend to supply missing words when we read our own writing, or because we know what intonation we intended, it is helpful to have another person read our compositions to us.

Sentence Length
Have students count the words in each sentence of a composition. Explain that when all the sentences are the same length, the writing may be monotonous. Provide examples to show students how skilled authors vary sentence length, resulting in a pleasant effect. As editors, students should rewrite some of their sentences to achieve this variety.

Spelling Check
Show students how to read their writing word by word, beginning with the last word! Because they are no longer paying attention to the meaning, they will notice spelling errors more accurately. They can do this for each other, too.

Interesting Words
Talk about words that are used often but that are not very interesting, such as "nice," "good," and "pretty." Give students several sentences such as the following:

>Mary is pretty.
>Kirk is nice.
>This book is good.

Suggest a way to rewrite each sentence. For example, instead of "Mary is pretty," you might write "Mary has curly red hair and a sparkle in her eye." Have students close their eyes and visualize the two sentences to compare the images they conjure. Encourage them to suggest alternative sentences to the one you rewrote. Point out how the image changes with each newly rewritten sentence. Also point out how clear an image becomes as more interesting detail is added.

Literature Models
Point out "beautiful sentences" that you observe in literature. As you find examples of particularly effective writing—especially descriptive sentences—write the examples on strips of paper. Display these strips on a bulletin board. Encourage students to share examples of "beautiful sentences" they have found.

As you read stories aloud, stop periodically when you notice a passage that contains effective description. Ask students to visualize the scenes described. Give them an opportunity to consciously observe the author's use of words to create a certain picture.

The Lesson Generator

This book provides you with a nucleus for a strong writing program that will carry you and your students through the school year. On the following pages, you will find a "Lesson Generator," which lists ideas to help you create more exciting writing lessons to supplement the ones in this book.

First, select any stimulus listed in Column 1. The stimuli are grouped in the following categories: short stories, films, children's books, poetry, and art. The stimulus may be considered a prewriting activity.

Then, from Column 2, decide on the type of main activity you want students to experience. The main activity is almost always a writing activity. It may also be an oral activity that supports the goals of the writing program.

In Column 3, we offer suggestions for following up a main activity. This column lists various ways of having students develop their writing. Finally, Column 4 suggests evaluation techniques you may wish to try.

The wonderful thing about the Lesson Generator is that it encourages you to keep adding to the list. For example, you probably know of other stories and short books you can use to stimulate writing. Also, you may think of other categories of stimuli, such as field trips or observing objects. Keep jotting notes on this chart to remind you of interesting possibilities. You, too, can create SAFE lessons!

The Lesson Generator

Stimulus

Short Stories

"Zlateh, the Goat", by Isaac Singer

"The Doughnuts", by Roger McCloskey

Petronella, by Jay Williams

Films

Rainshower
   Churchill

String Bean
   McGraw-Hill

Children's Books

I Love My Mother, by Paul Zindel

How to Go About Laying an Egg, by Bernard Waber

Poetry

"Richard Cory", by E. A. Robinson

"Arithmetic", by Carl Sandburg

Where the Sidewalk Ends, by Shel Silverstein

Art

Study a famous painting, sculpture, or other piece of art.

ADD YOUR OWN IDEAS HERE.

Activity

Retell a story from different points of view.

Prepare a story for Readers' Theater.

Write poems using a word, syllable, or rhyme pattern.

Write poems based on literature.

Copy dialogue from a book.

Write dialogue for a wordless book or film.

Write a children's book.

Write a paragraph in the style of a given author.

Write a paragraph explaining what you like about a book.

Read folktales and select one for retelling.

Write an essay about a piece of art.

ADD YOUR OWN IDEAS HERE.

Follow-up

Share stories in small groups.

Read in pairs.

Illustrate reports.

Compile stories or poems into booklets.

Make a class "Big Book," compiling stories or poems by everyone in the class.

Create a school magazine.

Act out a dialogue.

Display student-written books at a book fair.

Tell stories to other classes.

Plan a Readers' Theater assembly.

Display essays on the bulletin board.

ADD YOUR OWN IDEAS HERE.

Evaluation

Teacher observation

Group evaluation according to criteria set by the class

Self-evaluation

Flow-chart questions

Student-teacher conferences

Cassette-taped readings

Editorial committee

Performance in front of a small group, the entire class, or other classes

Audience response

Proofreading

Holistic scoring

Analytical reading

Group discussion

ADD YOUR OWN IDEAS HERE.

Children's Books Cited in This Text

Unit 1

Kellogg, Steven. *Can I Keep Him?* Dial, 1971.

Barrett, Judith. *Animals Should Definitely Not Wear Clothing.* Atheneum, 1970.

Fisher, Aileen. *You Don't Look Like Your Mother, Said the Robin to the Fawn.* Bowmar-Noble, 1973.

Unit 2

Van Allsburg, Chris. *Jumanji.* Houghton Mifflin, 1981.

Unit 3

Keats, Ezra Jack. *The Snowy Day.* Viking, 1962.

Martin, Bill, Jr. *Brown Bear, Brown Bear, What Do You See?* Holt, 1983.

Hutchins, Pat. *Changes, Changes.* Macmillan, 1971.

Mayer, Mercer. *A Boy, a Dog, and a Frog.* Dial, 1967.

Wezel, Peter. *The Good Bird.* Harper, 1966

Aruego, Jose. *Look What I Can Do.* Scribner, 1971.

Bolliger-Savelli, Antonella. *The Knitted Cat.* Macmillan, 1971.

Krahn, Fernando. *A Flying Saucer Full of Spaghetti.* Dutton, 1970.

Silverstein, Shel. *The Giving Tree.* Harper, 1964.

Charlip, Remy. *Fortunately.* Parents, 1964.

Emberly, Ed. *The Wing on a Flea: A Book About Shapes.* Little, 1961.

Unit 4

Yashima, Taro. *Umbrella.* Viking, 1958.

Unit 5

Schulz, Charles. *Happiness Is a Warm Puppy.* Determined Prods., 1983.

Mayer, Mercer. *There's a Nightmare in My Closet.* Dial, 1968.

Viorst, Judith. *Alexander and the Terrible, Horrible, No Good, Very Bad Day.* Atheneum, 1972.

Unit 7

Lobel, Arnold. *Fables.* Harper, 1980.

Reading Aloud

Here is a list of good books to share with your students. Through reading aloud, you teach your students to read, to think, and to write. As they listen, students learn about:

- grammar
- writing style
- imagery and figurative language
- new ideas or new ways to express ideas
- the joy of a good book

Always have a good book going in your classroom. Plan time for the students to think about what the class has read together.

Aardema, Verna. *Why Mosquitoes Buzz in People's Ears: A West African Tale*. Dial, 1975.

Bemelmans, Ludwig. *Madeline's Rescue*. Viking, 1953.

Brown, Marcia and Perrault, Charles. *Cinderella*. Scribner, 1954.

Brown, Marcia. *Once a Mouse*. Scribner, 1961.

Burton, Virginia Lee. *The Little House*. Houghton Mifflin, 1942.

Cendrars, Blaise. *Shadow*. Scribner, 1982.

Cooney, Barbara and Chaucer, Geoffrey. *Chanticleer and the Fox*. Crowell, 1958.

d'Aulaire, Ingrid and Edward. *Abraham Lincoln*. Doubleday, 1957.

De Regniers, Beatrice S. *May I Bring a Friend?* Atheneum, 1964.

Emberly, Barbara. *Drummer Hoff*. Prentice-Hall, 1967.

Ets, Marie Hall and Labastida, Aurora. *Nine Days to Christmas*. Viking, 1959.

Field, Rachel. *Prayer for a Child*. Macmillan, 1941.

Goble, Paul. *The Girl Who Loved Wild Horses*. Bradbury, 1978.

Hader, Berta and Elmer. *The Big Snow*. Macmillan, 1948.

Haley, Gail E. *A Story, A Story*. Atheneum, 1970.

Hall, Donald. *Ox-Cart Man*. Viking, 1979.

Handforth, Thomas. *Mei Li*. Doubleday, 1938.

Hodges, Margaret. *Saint George and the Dragon*. Little, 1984.

Hogrogian, Nonny. *One Fine Day*. Macmillan, 1971.

Langstaff, John and Rojankovsky, Feodor. *Frog Went A-Courtin'*. Harcourt, 1955.

Lawson, Robert. *They Were Strong and Good*. Viking, 1940.

Lipkind, William. *Finders Keepers*. Harcourt, 1951.

MacDonald, Golden. *The Little Island*. Doubleday, 1946.

McCloskey, Robert. *Make Way for Ducklings*. Viking, 1941.

McCloskey, Robert. *Time of Wonder*. Viking, 1957.

McDermott, Gerald. *Arrow to the Sun: A Pueblo Indian Tale*. Viking, 1974.

Milhous, Katherine. *The Egg Tree*. Scribner, 1950.

Mosel, Arlene. *The Funny Little Woman*. Dutton, 1972.

Musgrove, Margaret. *Ashanti to Zulu: African Traditions*. Dial, 1976.

Ness, Evaline. *Sam, Bangs & Moonshine*. Holt, 1966.

Nic Leodhas, Sorche (Alger, Leclaire). *Always Room for One More*. Holt, 1965.

Petersham, Maud and Miska. *Rooster Crows*. Macmillan, 1946.

Politi, Leo. *Song of the Swallows*. Scribner, 1949.

Provensen, Alice and Martin. *The Glorious Flight Across the Channel with Louis Bleriot*. Viking, 1983.

Ransome, Arthur. *The Fool of the World and the Flying Ship*. Farrar, Straus & Giroux, 1968.

Robbins, Ruth. *Baboushka and the Three Kings*. Parnassus, 1960.

Sendak, Maurice. *Where the Wild Things Are*. Harper, 1963.

Spier, Peter. *Noah's Ark*. Doubleday, 1977.

Thurber, James. *Many Moons*. Harcourt, 1943.

Tresselt, Alvin. *White Snow, Bright Snow*. Lothrop, 1947.

Udry, Janice. *A Tree Is Nice*. Harper, 1956.

Ward, Lynd. *Biggest Bear*. Houghton Mifflin, 1952.

Zemach, Harve. *Duffy and the Devil*. Farrar, Straus & Giroux, 1973.